eric
parry architects

e
pa

volume 2

black dog
publishing
london uk

Introduction
Dalibor Vesely

The second volume of Eric Parry Architects (EPA) works is a continuation and to a certain degree a fulfilment of the main intention, discussed in the first volume as a design situated in the "grey zone of modernity". The grey zone of modernity was identified as a gap between the culture of personal, introverted experience and the sphere of shared, but highly abstract culture, dominated by instrumental thinking. The choice to operate in this gap was motivated by an awareness, that the gap, if it is recognised as a problem and challenge, reveals the presence of a latent culture, which can serve as a foundation for a different kind of design.

The work of EPA, accomplished so far, illustrates the development of such a different kind of design which may be described as situational. The term "situational design" should not be confused with a simple reference to a given or chosen context. It is a more serious effort to situate each design task in a corresponding sphere of culture and place, manifested in the typicality of human situations. Typical situations represent the most complete way of understanding not only the nature of particular human tasks and events but also the corresponding experience of the surrounding world and the human qualities of the world that belong to them.

In the more recent projects, illustrated in this volume, the situational approach became gradually more focused on the deeper dimensions of situations—the conditions of their embodiment. This is not entirely surprising. Architectural understanding of situations leads inevitably to the discovery of their materiality and corporeality. The question of materiality of architecture is not new. It was discussed passionately particularly in the time of the avant-gardes and was given very often a misleading importance in design. The source of the "misleading importance" was, (and to some extent still is) a narrow understanding of materiality seen as a question of material, expressed in the well known cliché "truth to material". Truth meant almost exclusively a reference to the material essence of the material itself seen as universal in its behaviour, use and appearance. This can be best described as architectural positivism, which ignores the simple fact that material is always situated (and cannot exist otherwise). It is quite obvious that glass, steel or ceramics in the bathroom are very different from the same materials on the facade of a large building in the city. The difference is defined in each case by the nature of a particular corresponding situation. The relation of material and the nature of situations is not easy to understand and yet it is more important than we usually think. Understanding becomes nevertheless possible and easier if we look at the materiality of situations as a problem of corporeality and embodiment. In such a view the body of architecture ceases to be an inert mass and appears as a corporeal structure of different degrees of density, from the light of transparency to the darkness of foundations.

What holds the different degrees of density together is the unity of space. The unity of space depends on the continuity of references, which in our case is the continuity of embodiment understood not as the materiality of a particular part of a building but rather as situations and participations in the movement culminating in the ultimate reference to earth. How is this reference to the terrestrial reality and order mediated through the space? The process of mediation is revealed in our imagination and has its source in the differentiated materiality of the building. Gaston Bachelard describes this role of imagination as "material".

"Material imagination", he writes, "this amazing need for participation which, going beyond the attraction of the imagination of forms, thinks matter, dreams in it, lives in it or in other words materialises the imaginary…. Whenever images appear in series they point to a primal matter, a fundamental element."

The ability of imagination to materialise the imaginary has many implications and consequences. It can serve as an important criterion to assess the possibilities and limits of simulations, virtual realities, modelling etc.. It can also help us to understand the corporeal nature of abstract concepts and their link with the most elementary materials. The application of geometry in the cutting of stone is a good example. There is no doubt that architecture has been always shaped by abstract concepts, geometry and ideas, but never directly without mediation. It is difficult and rather problematic to realise a conceptual vision, diagram or abstract thought directly in a building. In design we spontaneously use a series of mediating steps such as drawings, models etc.. The mediated nature of abstract concepts or ideas in architecture can be seen in the examples of buildings with a plan formed as geometrical diagrams. It is true that both buildings and diagrams can be constructed by the same geometry. However in the case of buildings geometry does not serve a clearly and explicitly articulated form or meaning. In a building, geometry reflects the conditions of the site, the program and the overall spatial organisation. It is absorbed in the material and communicative nature of the space which is informed also by other media, but has itself the power to situate them. To situate means also to communicate. What communicates and what is communicated in architecture? For the lack of a better term, I am describing the enigmatic phenomenon of architectural communication as 'architectonic' structure, which is based on the already mentioned continuity of different levels of embodiment and reference to earth (terrestrial reality and order). Architectonic structure replaces the conventional term tectonics, a relatively modern invention which reduced the corporeal and communicative nature of space into a material structure defined usually by nothing more than a contract with gravity. Architectonics may replace not only tectonics, but also the popular reference to the 'architecture' of mathematics, music, literature, language, etc.. From our point of view the most interesting is the extension of architectonics into the sphere of language understood in its broadest sense.

The interpretation of a brief, potentially relevant to all elements of the building, reveals the tension between the anonymity and silence of the architectural body, including the visibility of the result that can be anticipated and verbal nature of the brief. This tension is characteristic for the whole history of architecture, particularly for the iconoclastic periods. The universality of the imagination that plays a dominating role in the visual arts is co-extensive with the universality of language. Like language, it can transform the material image into a pictorial one and eventually into the iconicity of abstract diagrams and concepts. How can imagination communicate between such different levels of reality and different areas of culture as architecture, sculpture, painting, language, music or dance? This is still little understood. The role of material imagination and its close links with language may help us here.

In a less-known private revelation, Marcel Proust confided that his *A la Recherche du Temps Perdu* can be compared to a cathedral. He was not referring to a formal analogy between his text and the structure of a cathedral but to the intimate link between the narrative, embodied in the written text, and the deeply embodied anticipation of writing in stone. In a different place he is more explicit:

"And in all the stone's veins and bones and flame-like stainings, and broken and disconnected lines, they write various legends, never untrue, of the former political state, of the world to which they belonged, of its infirmities and fortitudes, convulsions and consolidations, from the beginning of time."

The corporeal and communicative understanding of space brings us closer to a better understanding and appreciation of the intentions behind such projects as the office building on Finsbury Square. Situated in the heart of the City the building responds to the abstract, calculative nature of the financial world and to the potential dignity and ethos of the civic world in the exterior of the building. Both worlds can be represented verbally and partly visually, but are also embodied in the physiognomy of the building. In view of what we have said so far it is possible to claim that the silence of embodiment is always to a certain extent also a voice of articulation.

This brings our argument very close to Heidegger's effort to grasp the reciprocity between the articulated world and its embodiment, which he describes as 'earth'. In his view of the work of art, "the setting up a world, does not cause the material to disappear, but rather causes it to come forth for the very first time and to come to the open of the works world. The rock comes to bear and rest and so first becomes rock; metals come to glitter and shimmer, colours to glow, tones to sing, the word to speak. All this comes forth as the work sets itself back into the massiveness and heaviness of stone, into the firmness and pliancy of wood, into the hardness and luster of metal, into the lighting and darkening of colour, into the clang of tone, and into the naming power of the word." The reciprocity of the heaviness of stone and the naming power of word is reflected in the office building on Finsbury Square as a reciprocity of the corporeality of stone and world, represented by geometry and light.

The nature of the building is most clearly revealed in the physiognomy of the west facade. Its configuration oscillates between the structural requirements absorbed in the overall geometry of the facade and the spatial considerations focused on the depth of the facade and the orchestration of light.

In the final solution both structure and geometry are subordinated to the structuring power of light and yet some tension between light and geometry remains. This is not surprising once we realise that throughout history architectural space was structured either by light or by geometry, sometimes by their ambiguity.

In the post-Cartesian world geometry dominates but earlier it was light that dominated the structure of space. This understanding of the nature of space is slowly returning as can be seen in the classical definition of architecture by Le Corbusier: "Architecture is a learned game, correct and magnificent, of forms assembled in the light."

In the Gothic cathedral, structured by geometry to the last detail, stone was elevated to serve the formation of the space of ultimate light. The formation of space by light is well described in contemporary text: "Light", the text claims, "which is the first form created in the first matter (*prima forma corporalis*), multiplied itself by its very nature an infinite number of times on all sides and spread itself out uniformly in every direction. In this way it proceeded in the beginning of time to extend matter which it could not leave behind by drawing it out along with itself into a mass the size of a material universe. How closely light was associated with matter in the late Middle Ages can be seen in the references to the presence of light in such elementary bodies or matter as minerals, stone or coal. The fascination with the luminosity of certain minerals, precious stones or glass made out of dust-like material, illustrates the power of light in a particular culture."

This brings us close to the treatment of the renovation of St Martin-in-the-Fields and Church Path. Most of the changes and their content are accommodated in spaces defined by light. In the nave of the church it is an evenly distributed light, which reveals the original luminosity of the row of columns differentiated from their capital and few other elements, including the apsis, leaving the vault floating separately above as if in a distant, transcendental light. In the crypt the light is reflected from the darker masonry confirming its subterranean material density. In contrast the spaces of the entrance pavilion and lightwell in the Church Path are structured as transparent in terms of visibility and penetrating light. The transparency culminates in the window glass in the church, most clearly in the stained glass window of the east wall.

The stained glass windows are a useful reminder that light and vision cannot be understood in separation from the luminous world. What light brings to visibility is a physiognomy of a particular scene and setting, formed always by a corresponding programme and content.

One of the best qualitative understanding of light in glass windows is available already in a classical text from the time of the cathedrals, which describes the action of light in the following way—"when a ray passes through a medium of strongly-coloured glass or crystal or cloth, there appears to us in the dark in the vicinity of the ray a colour similar to the colour of that strongly-coloured body; and this colour is an opaque substance that intercepts it, is called the 'similitude and species' of the colour in the strongly-coloured body through which the ray passes". The role of light in the formation of space particularly in relation to its corporeality opens the door to a better understanding of its true communicative nature which includes also other media, such as language, music, dance, etc..

This is particularly relevant in projects of such subtlety and complexity as the Music School in Bedford. If we continue to reveal the way of thinking, hidden behind the projects, as we have done so far, we come across the most important and provocative question—how does architecture in its corporeality come to terms with and contribute to the performance of the almost immaterial sound of music?

We realise how subtle the problem is when we discover that particular music does or does not belong to a particular space. In a space of a concert hall where the silence of architecture is complemented by the sound of music or words embodied in music we can recognise a distinct mode of spatiality in the sphere of music or words, performed, as it were, from the same page. We can discover the link between the reality of space and music owing to a reverberation which takes place on the boundary of the visual and acoustic space. At the first stage reverberation is like a melody played in different keys.

The phenomenon of reverberation brings to a new light the movement of imagination and the aspect of movement that makes imagination truly communicative. It is for this reason that Eugène Minkowski chose reverberation as a paradigm in his own studies of the formation of a poetic image. He describes reverberation in the following way: "If, having the original image in our mind's eye, we ask ourselves how that image comes alive and fills with life, we discover a new dynamic and vital category, a new property of the universe, reverberation. It is as though the sound of a hunting horn reverberating everywhere through its echo made the tiniest leaf, the tiniest wisp of moss shudder in a common movement and transform the whole forest, filling it to its limits, into a vibrating, sonorous world.... It is the dynamism of the sonorous life itself which by engulfing and appropriating everything it finds in its path, fills the slice of space, or better the slice of the world that it assigns itself by its movement, making it reverberate, breathing into it its own life."

The role of reverberation in the formation of a poetic image is represented in the case of the Music School by the power of music to animate the image and the body of architectural space and the power of space to contribute to the nature of music. This double movement brings to light one of the main general characteristics of architecture, its apparent silence complemented by a close link with the more explicitly articulated strata of culture.

The extension and cultivation of the link between the corporeality of architectural space and the more explicitly articulated strata of culture has been the most characteristic concern of the EPA office in their recent projects and remains the main task for the future.

Detail of glazed brick wall at Wimbledon School of Art. Artist, John Mitchell.

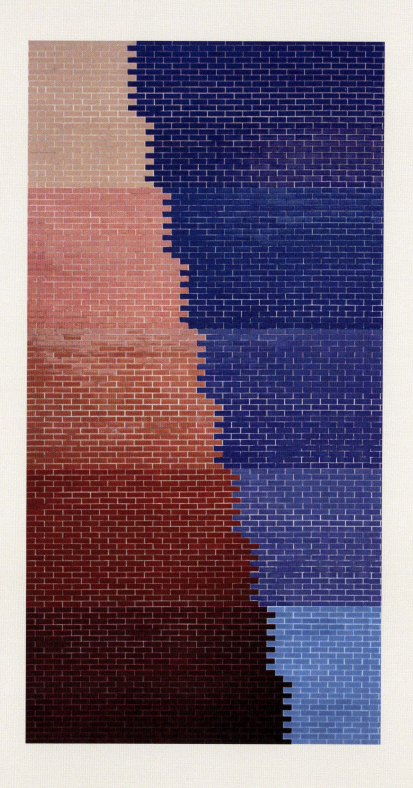

Corporeality
On the recent work
Wilfried Wang

Even with the debilitating fixation of free market economies on the rapid return on investments, the ever-greater insistence by some architectural media on novelty and photogenicity, and the reduction in choice in constructional details there is space for decent architecture. In this context, decent meaning: fitting, worthy, well formed and marked by moral integrity.

The socio-cultural context, in which the work of Eric Parry Architects is set, is arguably one of contemporary civilisation's most laden with contradictions. London, to be more precise: the City of London, one of the world's leading financial centres that remains unassailed by its pauperised neighbours; London: the cradle of anachronistic pageant and the paradigm of pragmatism that pretends to be value-free; England: the country that forever wants to tell others, especially foreigners, how they should lead their lives but that forever opts out of more shared values if these values come from the (European) outside; there remain possibilities for the intellectual freedom and the cultural enterprise for patient architects and discerning clients.

Given the range of possibilities that architects can pursue, and the broad scope of architectural discourse embraced in Britain (ranging from the Victorian inspired love of technology to the usually Victorian origins of anti-machinist movements such as the Luddites), the territory that an architect chooses to occupy is ultimately determined by personal choice. Talent alone advances the individual, but equally, can fail the individual in highly differentiated, complex tasks. Talent needs to be augmented or completed by intellectual curiosity and its attendant research instruments.

Treading a delicate balance between abstraction's suggestive imagination and its modernist powers of essentialisation, the work of EPA searches for the corporeal in architecture. With this notion is meant the figured material presence constituted through interrelated constructional and tectonic elements creating spaces and configurations for human occupation and use.

Two aspects differentiate architecture from the other plastic arts in this search: first, the difficult possibility of material veracity, that is to say, can one be sure that what one sees constitutes firstly an edifice's structure and secondly, the infinite possibility of spatial creation? Corporeality in architecture does not end in the object-focused creative act; its complement is the creation of space and place. The obverse aspect of corporeality is the provision of a protected interior through the construction of covering envelopes.

In turn, the covering envelopes become the ambidextrous media for the representation and constitution of the created/supported space. Covering envelopes in this context are not mere skins, sheets

In-situ board-marked concrete water wall at 5 Aldermanbury Square.

or immaterial layers, but on the contrary, substantive structures. These structures are subject to a multitude of combinatorial rules, in the artistic sense: rules of composition; in the constructive sense: rules of connection. Contemporary practice on and off the building site highlights the increasing schism between these two senses. Between the outer and innermost skins, there are necessary, constitutive layers whose visible presence is short-lived. Each layer of construction is the domain of a specialist; without a principled insight into each of these special domains the contemporary architect increasingly plays on the sidelines.

Recognising this schism, EPA are exploring the nature and logic of covering envelopes. In the course of this exploration, in which the office building on Finsbury Square has offered the principle of accepting the differentiation of envelopes or layers and setting this as the concept for defining the rules of composition and construction, the separation of a building's layers has laid bare, so to speak, the possibility of returning to the full-bodied, that is corporeal nature of primary structure. What has been a theme or example in ancient Greek and Chinese architecture, that is, the use of peripteral or in-set (in antis) columns distinct from a masonry enclosure, finds a contemporary interpretation in the Finsbury Square office building. However, as opposed to the conventional two-dimensional role of cladding representing structure, the Finsbury Square office building retrieves a structural role for the peripteral pillars. The loadbearing pillars are thus a case of tectonics becoming plastic, that is three-dimensional.

The explorations in the possibilities of plastic tectonics engage the grand tradition of trabeated precedents, suggesting the conceptual continuity of the structural principles that have for millennia communicated the plausibility of a building's integrity.

While much of contemporary construction has become 'flat', mere images devoid of true physical consequences, EPA's projects consistently seek to unite the spatial and configurational possibilities within elegantly, that is not formally, attenuated but intelligently conceived construction.

Plastic tectonics, as a design strategy aimed as much at engaging the formal complexities of stratified sites, their embedded histories as well as the strands of architectural discipline, offers a conduit for buildings to regain their physicality.

In the context of twenty-first century London, physicality is not to be misunderstood as the brandishing of icons across the city's silhouette. It is rather the proximate experience of a building's constituent parts, the rationale for which is dictated both by the requirements of the programme and also by the often unarticulated demands of external expectations, historical values, contextual response and straightforward architectural intelligibility.

The work of EPA is far from the mute self-sufficiency of late purism. Here is no denial of joints and materiality, on the contrary, demonstrating the wisdom of ancient masons, exquisite blocks of stone are placed limpidly on top of each or side by side. Steel panels of giant dimensions are aligned in such a way as to read simultaneously as 'monoliths' as well as straightforward cladding, a nonchalant play on constructional knowledge and its formal effects.

Certainly, some parts of Parry's designs seem to recall purist compositional intentions. On closer inspection, however, the visible articulations are found to be an integral part of the ostensibly mute configuration's implicit constructional and tectonic conception.

The pursuit of plastic tectonics in architectural composition allows EPA to ground the work in a rationale informed by the orders, while remaining receptive to the wealth of precedents as exemplified in the work of Nicholas Hawksmoor, Balthasar Neumann, John Soane and Auguste Perret. In all of these works, walls, ceilings, beams, columns and piers give a brilliant sense of being legible both as principal objects before a secondary background and as reticent components of a greater whole. This sense of oscillation, of connecting different experiential worlds, from the physical material to the spatial abstract, removes the projects by EPA from the uni-dimensional realm of meaning.

The possibilities of plastic tectonics also encompasses a secondary spectrum of complex cladding details which in turn create a language of interlinking textures subtly informing a building's overall form. Thus glazing systems with their calibrated mullions and transoms, interlaced with subframes and ultimately tied together with the primary structure, can be read as veils or textile screens, with their own order of assembly, their own *architecture en miniature*.

From *l'architecture en miniature* to plastic tectonics both linear compositional relationships as well as superimposed or collaged compositions can result. The recent projects by EPA exhibit both aspects.

Elephant and Castle residential tower. Initial model from wood off-cuts.

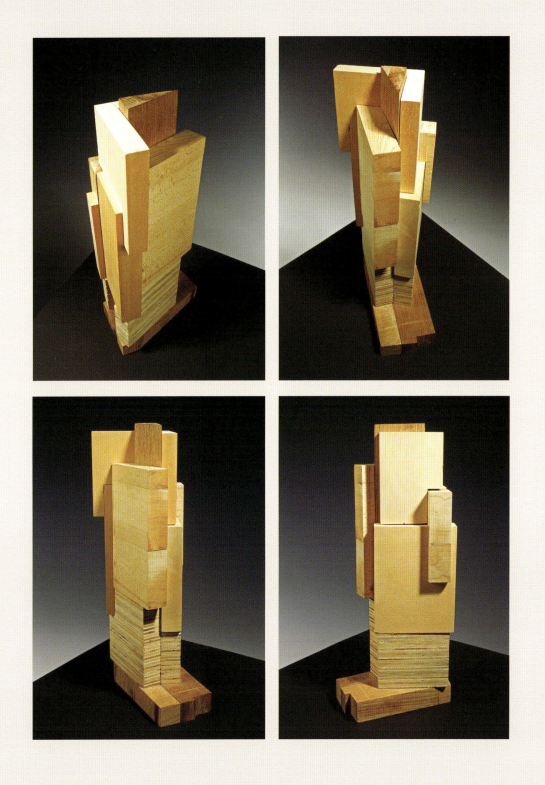

Predicated on a close reading of the physical and temporal context, the work of the practice rejects any self-sufficient late purism or ahistorical celebration of the latest technological advances. In this sense, EPA are quintessentially suited to work within the English landscape; one full of fearful anticipation of inevitable changes as well as of nervous anxiety in being left out of the benefits of progress.

EPA's gradually intensifying involvement in the socio-politically fraught City of London, the respect paid to the practice by official and semi-official conservation bodies and the range of commissions received from established middle-English institutions are all indicative of the distinguished role the practice plays in early twenty-first century England.

EPA's intelligible and intelligent approach creates the possibility of an architecture which connects and resolves the ostensibly immutable and unmovable.

5 Aldermanbury Square textile wall hangings in production on the loom.

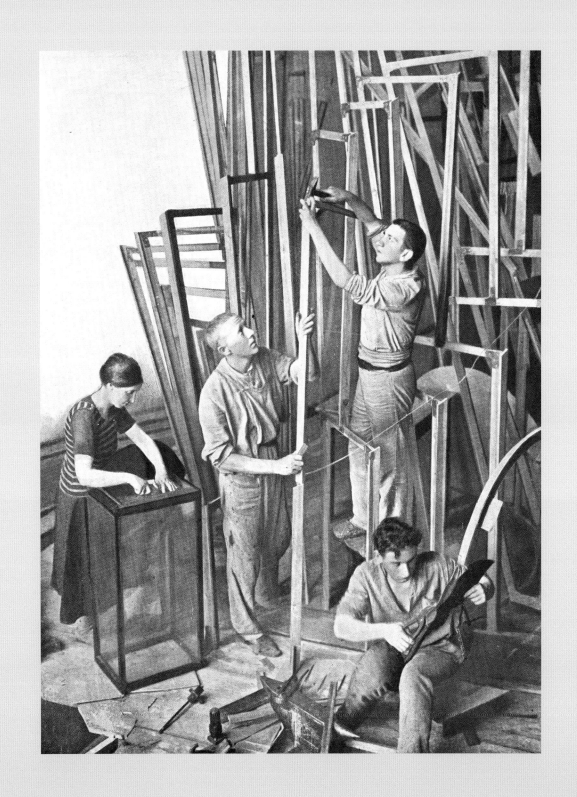

The English intellectual context

Normally, the two words "England" and "intellectual" do not appear comfortably in tandem.[1] While there has been no shortage of a form of literary criticism or exegesis appearing as architectural theory in the United States of America during the last two decades of the twentieth century, little has emerged from either side of the Atlantic in that period. The spectrum of the architectural discourse in England at the turn of the century has ranged from the light journalistic chatter of the tabloids (including daily and weekly media, of the latter type *Building Design* and *Blueprint*) to the occasional theoretical, if not esoteric reviews from some of the more ambitious academic institutions. Given the overwhelming presence of the English language, the relative absence of this discourse within the international scene is remarkable, more so, the complete absence of any sustained influence of "architectural thought"—that is, in union with built architecture—from England.

A partial explanation may be provided by the fact that from the early nineteenth century the English intellect appears to have been inextricably linked to a form of empiricism; in the realm of architecture this would, with seemingly ineluctable logic become embodied in a stubborn pragmatist attitude.[2] This attitude, combined with the increasingly sophisticated property-centric economy and an equally complex marketing and advertising machine fostered a real mistrust of real quality in architecture.

Eric Parry's teacher and friend Dalibor Vesely laments this state of affairs in his book *Architecture in the Age of Divided Representation*, exactly reflecting the depth of the intellectual discourse continuing in the minds of Eric Parry and his colleagues.[3]

One concern in the notion of divided representation is the possibility of physical, temporal and spatial atomisation of built phenomena.[4] Thus, the validity in the separation of the here and now of a phenomenon from its origins, sources and traditions, to give just one example, as had been propagated since the period of instrumentalised abstraction even as early as the beginnings of the enlightenment, has until today conserved the schism between an individual's claim to the freedom of creativity on the one hand and her or his obligation to the comprehension of a phenomenon's gestation on the other, let alone the presentation of such an understanding within an architectural design.

England, which was by comparison to continental Europe spared mass physical destruction during World War II, was subsequently devastated by the interventions of traffic engineers and town planners during the Wilson-inspired era of the 'white heat of technology', an uneasy mix of quixotic domestic fantasy and unindustrualised 'enlightenment'. Such unrequited and unresolved juxtapositions, to be found at the heart of many English conurbations and best viewed from railway viaducts or cuttings that inadvertently offer

Making. Vladimir Tatlin's *Monument to the Third International.* Model under construction, 1919.

a patchwork of that most private domain of English life—the back garden—seem to set the carefree precedent for later generations of engineers and architects. Jumps in scale, the harsh conflict of public and private aspiration, of noise and quiet, of financial and social values, in short, of deeply entrenched cultural differences, appear to be the context within which architects of a radical and modern persuasion could easily flourish.

The acknowledged pioneers of English modernism (that is the adherents of continental European modernism), from Berthold Lubetkin, the MARS Group, to the engineer Owen Williams, no doubt felt as equally liberate as the majority of their continental European counterparts from having to relate their building designs to any part of the topographic or built context. The locus of a building's *raison d'être* could be perceived to reside just within its programme. It was thought correct that a break with history, especially with its architectural branch, should take place. While an understanding of the classical orders—Doric, Ionic and Corinthian—were required until the 1960s in British schools of architecture, the notion of history was subsequently relegated as dispensable beginning with the interwar period. Thus, while the early English modernists and even the early post-World War II architects had a classical grounding, the diminishing interest in and appreciation of the plastic-sculptural qualities of architectural precedents based on the classical tradition would lead to the desensitisation of form-making, where form is understood to be dependent on the understanding of the meaning of each component within the whole.

Breaking with the past, with conventional history, with the grand traditions of architecture, would bring a compositional freedom that happily ignored the relationship between object and context, and the role that mouldings and joints—as constituent parts of composition—had played in the past. The atomisation of architectural designs would ultimately set apart the new from the old, would ignore the responsibility towards the whole even if the task is to design only a small part of a context. Setting buildings free from history and context would allow for the presentation of a new world, one in which society and individual could seemingly exist without the clutter of rites and rituals. Architecture and urban design served to fulfil this aspiration in presenting themselves liberated from their respective clutter: ornament and mouldings, streets and squares; instead: flush details and basic geometric shapes, streets-in-the-air and community centres.

Had modern architecture and town planning been given a free hand, no doubt much of the built substance carried over from the past, that is, from pre-modernist times, would have given way to wholesale 'modernisation', even if dressed in a range of styles in the immediate post-war years.[5] Such a thesis may sound extreme at first, but given the palpably ongoing, apparently unstoppable building activity in the financial district of London—the City of London, its validity can easily be proven. Within the City of London's so-called "Square Mile", over three quarters of the built fabric has been replaced since 1945, most of this with a visible outward presence.[6] A similar process is readable in other parts of London. What is the cultural consequence of this creeping, unacknowledged and continuing replacement of built fabric of which both the general public and the profession is largely unaware?

As shall be seen in the discussion on EPA's contribution to Paternoster Square, itself a historically-laden fragment of the City of London immediately north of St Paul's Cathedral, the once pioneering modernists, who saw themselves in the role of the underdogs, would in turn become the victims of a similar 'modern' wholesale replacement strategy. While William Holford's plan for Paternoster Square, 1961–1967, was expressly designed for office use only, represented as such in a homogeneous architecture, the extent and relentlessness of the latter became the source of its own demise. Clearly fed-up with this kind of grim modernism, the possibility of the redevelopment of Paternoster Square fired the imagination of the pendulum swingers in the guise of the constant king-to-be and his architectural advisers.

The Paternoster Square masterplan by William Whitfield of 1996, more so than any other large urban project in Britain, established the linguistic consensus for urban proposals of subsequent decades. London had already seen large-scale redevelopments of British Rail property (for example smaller scale schemes at London Bridge, Charing Cross, and Cannon Street stations, as well as large-scale projects at Broadgate/Liverpool Street and King's Cross/St Pancras stations) for office use, in which numerous architects participated. Such a variety in appearances within a given masterplan found the support of decision makers and the public alike: it played to the general imagination of what constitutes urban diversity regardless of use.

Reinterpreting the modernist dictum "form follows function", Paternoster Square is a paradigm for formal diversity despite functional homogeneity. The City of London, before World War II the real place of abode for

5 Aldermanbury Square, detail of the northwest corner.

over a hundred thousand inhabitants, now with a few thousand residents, is playing 'city'. While, for counter-example, planning rules in Berlin following post-1990 reunification required at least 20 per cent residential use for each inner city development, such strictures would not be countenanced in the home of free enterprise. What had been a tourist success in London's Covent Garden Market (the market function having been moved by the then GLC in 1973 to Nine Elms) in the 1980s, served as a model for inner city rehabilitation and conservation in the 1990s not only for English towns. Covent Garden retained some of its urban culture, that is, its functional diversity with some residences, albeit in the normative, defensible and convoluted housing estates, and mostly offices and retail uses. The urban design image was transposed to other developments in London, notably the aforementioned railway sites and the City of London as a whole.

London, Steen Eiler Rasmussen's ideal of a civilised and enlightened polis, holds few examples of late twentieth, let alone early twenty-first century urban design culture, where the word culture means the integral whole of both behavioural patterns and creative manifestations. Where urban culture seems to be newly integrated, as in the case of the Paternoster Square development, there are only office clerks and tourists. Where it appears to endure, as in Covent Garden, there has been a successful takeover of the original market by the international retailing trade. The forces of the modern economy—the financial markets and tourism—have displaced the urban culture that existed in the above sense of culture prior to World War II. It is in this context of make-believe, that the architecture of EPA is to be viewed. Beyond the simple debates about style then, there is the question as to whether EPA's concern for corporeality, amongst others, is the matrix by which their architectural designs are moulded to integrate the new within the existing, to present a frame through which a user can begin to understand the history (here understood as an enduring impression of values, behavioural patterns and creative manifestations) of a particular place.

London today, some eight decades after Rasmussen's accolade of the uniqueness of the city's fabric, the result of the lives of its people, is suffering from the myopic 'vision' of traffic engineers who are held on a short leash, permitted to regulate vehicular traffic by means of a combination of 'sleeping policemen' (or speed bumps), lane width reductions, the 'congestion charge' (or toll charge) and complex one-way traffic routes with punitive consequences for the ignorant. London at the beginning of the twenty-first century is, besides New York City, one of the destinations for the property collector with a pattern of short-term visits. Investors from everywhere have sought and are continuing to seek places to live. The forces of jet-set society, parallel to the financial market and tourism, are displacing traditional residents. The prospect of life in a commuter region, that lacks both modernised public transport and an efficient regional rail service, holds increasing journey times for all.[7] The planned Crossrail network, connecting Maidenhead to Shenfield and Abbey Wood through central London by 2015, albeit north of the Thames, will undoubtedly reduce some of the transport pressure in and across London.

The absence of both political foresight and to some extent political power in order, to radically reorganise the London mass transport system, which by example Paris had implemented with its RER system from 1962 to 1977, is mirrored by the hands-off approach to urban densification by both central and local government. Public or council housing has effectively ceased its construction programme since the implementation of the restrictive local government reforms of the last consecutive Conservative governments, 1979–1997; since then the Labour government has only belatedly, through the office of London's Mayor and organisations such as English Partnerships and the Housing Corporation, to deliver sufficient supply of affordable inner city housing, although collaboration with the private sector is starting to make some impact.

Rasmussen's London, expansive as it was already in the 1930s, has at the beginning of the twenty-first century become a region the extent of Los Angeles. Public transport and housing, key issues for the viability, let alone the quality of life, of a city, are straining under these pressures. This forms the broad context of EPA's practice. Whereas the social concern that architects had, and some still have, would bring them closer to public commissions, in the absence of such visions and projects, the range of buildings contained in this volume of EPA's work gives a fair cross-section of typical commissions realised by architects in England at the beginning of the twenty-first century.

London, once a unique city, is now an advertising hoarding, a billboard that speaks of quaint Englishness, anachronistic royalty, bull-doggish football, abstruse money cycling, cross-cultural minstrels, aggressive art collecting and extraordinary witty creativity. Each facet of this hoarding overwhelms and yet contributes little of long-lasting value to

Urban Necropolis, St Giles, London. Project 1979.

the physical reality of the city, quite unlike the process that Rasmussen described almost a century ago. Pursuing the corporeal in architecture must be seen as a cultural critique of this billboard situation.

Ron and Andrew Herron, some two years after Robert Venturi, Denise Scott Brown and Steven Izenour's *Learning from Las Vegas* launched a scathing attack on the Bauhaus-mentality of the dominant East Coast and European architecture scene, demystified the English suburban dream of the very private life behind the uniform facades of the semi-detached half-timbered homes: "Behind the public facade exists the crank, misfit and eccentric, and the whole range of taste prevails—fed by advertising and the media."[8] Distinct then from the Las Vegas 'building board', where content and label are separated to each efficiently perform their assigned tasks, the Herronesque 'suburban set' is an insulating mask, protecting idiosyncratic privacy. It is the strength of this Anglo-Saxon instance of individuation that knows how to maintain social appearances behind uniforms, of which Adolf Loos had already commented in his essay "Ornament and Crime" of 1908: "The person who runs around in a velvet suit is no artist but a buffoon or merely a decorator. We have become more refined, more subtle. Primitive men had to differentiate themselves by various colours; modern man needs his clothes as a mask. His individuality is so strong that it can no longer be expressed in terms of items of clothing."[9]

The consequences of these insights on the separation of content from the means of representation in architecture, from Vienna via Las Vegas to the suburbs of England, are that the division of design labour at the beginning of the twenty-first century implies for most practicing architects a diminished sphere of work. While buildings cannot but remain plastic, three-dimensional, what is sought from architects is increasingly a signature mask that prints well. The concentration of the architectural statement to a few square inches in a coloured journal parallels the willing acceptance by many users that the experiential sequence from the public space via a building's exterior through to its interior is either completely irrelevant, that the lack of integrity is not even noticed, or that these sometimes irreconcilable differences are to be expected.

The dissolution of a coherent experience of what constitutes cities and architecture, either through post-World War II zoning laws as seen everywhere across the world and distinctly in the City of London, or through the greedy taxidermy of a building's inner structure or even their wholesale replacement, depends to a large degree on the fast track logic of an ever-rising property market.[10] This logic has no face. It uses the mask of billboards, facades and townscapes to provide the game board of contemporary life. It is much closer to the first version of *Second Life* than most people realise.

In this context, what role and hope for the corporeal? Architectural computer programs eliminate issues of materiality and construction. The continuity of pixels is their goal. The rules of geometry, which are abstract and entirely autonomous from the realities of construction and gravity, determine the assembly of surfaces and light in CAD programs. Points have no weight, lines and planes no thickness; and yet in concert they simulate mass, material and form.

Over the centuries, architects have given increasing credibility to geometry, as if architecture's life depended on it. In civilisations in which geometry as a science only plays a marginal role, building has still come into being, creating complex shapes at that. The ingenuity of the Inuit in their construction of domes or that of the native North American Indians (e.g. the Mi'kmag tribe) or Vikings in the construction of vessels gives evidence of the primacy of the act of construction over the theoretical abstraction through the act of geometrical contemplation.

In this essay, the corporeal in architecture is conceived as the real presence of material facts constituting the conceptual and sensual ground by which the spatial and formal being of a work of architecture can be understood by a user. Thus the corporeal in architecture is neither to be reduced to the fetishistic 'body'—discourse (and in its wake, the formalist compositional debate), nor is it to be seen simply as a return to classical metaphors in which components of architecture, or indeed a work of architecture as a whole, are projections of human or animal figures.

[1] See, for instance, the investigation by Stefan Collini, *Absent Minds: Intellectuals in Britain*, Oxford, 2006, in which the myth of English anti-intellectualism is analysed: While "it is not... the English character which is averse to thought; we are not the plain practical people that we boast... to be", (JR Seeley's rebuttal of Collini's thesis of "absence"), it is the notion that pragmatism and empiricism are if not distant from continental European intellectualism then at least distinct exceptions to it.

[2] From this nineteenth century attitude has survived the mechanistic aspect of Victorian engineering as can be seen in the work of the Richard Rogers Partnership, Michael Hopkins & Partners, or Grimshaw Architects.

[3] Vesely, Dalibor, *Architecture in the Age of Divided Representation: The Question of Creativity in the Shadow of Production*, Cambridge, MA, 2004.

[4] Vesely, *Architecture in the Age of Divided Representation*, p. 20.

[5] For instance, so-called post-war town planning was already being undertaken both in Britain and Germany during World War II. The 1943/44 Abercrombie plans suggested a number of interlinked open spaces throughout London. Similar plans were being drawn for small and large towns in Germany, see for instance Jörn Düwel, et al, *1945 Krieg–Zerstörung–Aufbau, Architektur und Stadtplanung 1940–1960*, Berlin, 1995.

[6] See for example an analysis published in 1992 by the author of the age of buildings in three adjoining London boroughs: "Camden South, the County and City of London and the Isle of Dogs: A Mapping of three areas in England, *Tradición y Cambio en la Arquitectura de seis Ciudades Europeas*, Madrid, 1992, pp. 55–76.

[7] Ripley, Amanda, et al, "The Cars that ate London, Paris, Brussels, Amsterdam, Rome, Madrid, Vienna, Athens", *Time Magazine*, 16 February 2003, http://www.time.com/time/magazine/article/0,9171,901030224-423479-2,00.html.

[8] Venturi, Robert, Denise Scott Brown, Steven Izenour, *Learning from Las Vegas*, Cambridge, MA, 1972.

In Andrew and Ron Herron "Suburban Sets", 1974–1975, three examples of private lives behind the same facades are credibly illustrated: the modern architect who has turned the conventional plot into a modern house complete with grass roof; the airstream camping family who have substituted the original house with a life pod; and the most extreme case of the retired bomber pilot who lives in a World War II "Liberator" bomber, which takes up the entire plot. Andrew and Ron Herron, "Suburban Sets", *A Question of Style*, ed. W Wang, London, 1978, p. 22.

[9] Loos, Adolf, "Ornament und Verbrechen", *Sämtliche Schriften*, vol. 1, ed. Franz Glück, Vienna, 1962, p. 288; English trans, *The Architecture of Adolf Loos*, ed. Yehuda Safran and Wilfried Wang, London, 1985, p. 103.

[10] The London domestic and commercial property market is one of the fastest growing in the world. The Nationwide Building Society's Index in March 2007 showed a growth from June 2004 to March 2007 of nearly 40 per cent in prime and mainstream London properties.

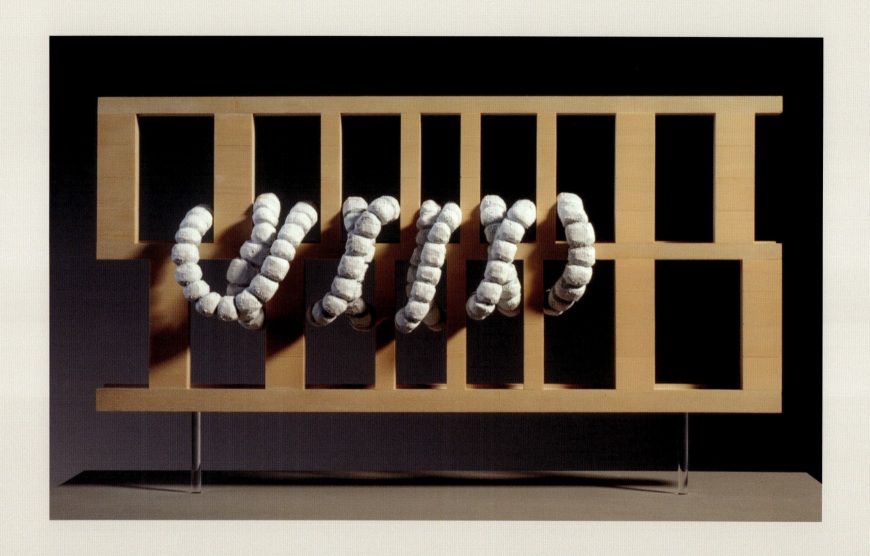

The difficulties and obligations of the corporeal in architecture

To pretend that today the realisation of architecture with palpable physicality can be achieved with ease, would be to misunderstand the history of the division of knowledge, labour and consequently of the crafts (including those in construction). In times of constrained resources which challenged ingenuity the covering shell was constituted by a single material, and therefore made by relatively restricted crafts. The so-called "primitive hut", whether made of animal (the tent or yurt), mineral (the vaulted earthen hut) or vegetal (the Caribbean hut) materials were restricted by relying on local resources. With off-site manufacture of building components and ever further reaching methods of transport, the maturation of which may be associated with the period of industrialisation, the notion of locality in culture could be diluted or altogether transcended. The stricture of the origin of building materials in times of cheap labour, materials and transport has not been relevant to broader architectural discourse for some time.

Undoubtedly, prior to the modern period of the mid-eighteenth century, the transportability of ideas and forms had already been easy and ubiquitous practice in the fields of crafts and fine arts by trading communities such as the Phoenicians (for example). Extraordinary efforts to transport building materials were undertaken for monuments, temples and tombs throughout recorded history. What characterised their extraordinariness was the very excess in labour that was expended in gathering heavy building materials such as large blocks of stone or rare tree trunks at a distant building site. The descriptions in the Bible of the construction of King Solomon's Temple give a good insight into such awe-inspiring excesses.

Equally, there are cases of private homes at the beginning of the twenty-first century, in which as a mark of distinction, both client and architect lay great emphasis on the extremes of material dimension. From wall depths in real stone to floorboards of solid timber, from single slabs of marble with enormous dimensions to thick planks of wood for dining tables, mass in minimalist form sets an aesthetic category. However, there is often a difference between the ostentatious representation of mass and the carefully calibrated integration of elements, albeit massive, within an architecture that deserves this name.

Corporeal architecture in the twenty-first century therefore must be seen in the context of the biblical romanticism on the one hand and the false modesty of minimalism on the other. The corporeal in architecture is the difficult obligation to both the constitution and representation of a built form in so far as each part should be taken and understood for what it is and, in a building's cumulative composition, in the manner in which these parts are gathered to synthesise the next order of comprehension: that of a building's figuration. When reference is made to an architecture's configuration, this morphological

Ceramic bead maquette. Unexecuted proposal by Richard Deacon for 30 Finsbury Square.

order of cognition allows for all the other components to recede into the background. Constructional and tectonic elements, so to speak, play supporting roles in the overall appearance of a building's resultant form, subsumable as the configuration. As a morphological category, configurations lead relatively independent existences within the spectrum of cognition.

The recent buildings by Eric Parry Architects display this relative independence. From the Library and Music School at Bedford to the entrance pavilion for St Martin-in-the-Fields, the architects have inserted recognisable architectural entities into grown contexts. The one exception, the office block for Paternoster Square, results from an amalgam of urban elements of William Whitfield's masterplan (softened rhomboidal site, colonnade) and set back requirements.

The following critique of the recently completed buildings by EPA will investigate the relation between corporeality of architecture and its cultural setting.

Turner Contemporary, Margate.

top: East elevation, dawn
bottom: South elevation, mid-day.

Pastel and pencil drawings of the proposed museum and the existing Droit House.

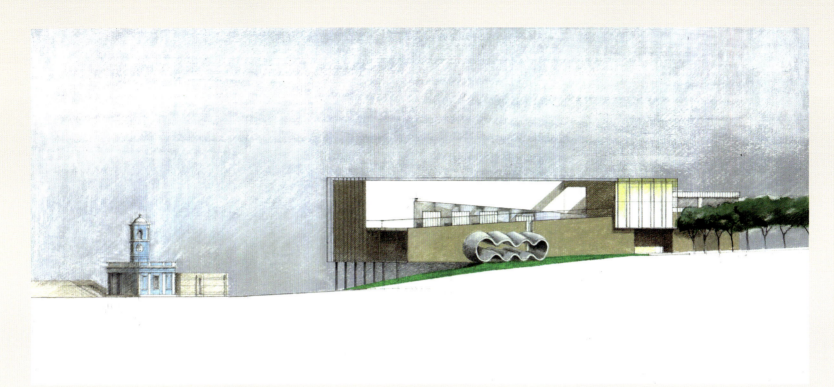

epa

volume 2

Contents

32	*30 Finsbury Square,* London
48	*Old Wardour House,* London
58	*London Residence,* London
70	*Royal Lancaster Hotel,* London
80	*London Stock Exchange,* London
92	*Bedford Library,* Bedford
104	*Bedford Music School,* Bedford
116	*Wimbledon School of Art,* Wimbledon
126	*Timothy Taylor Gallery,* London
134	*185 Park Street,* London
142	*5 Aldermanbury Square,* London
160	*Three London Offices,* London
168	*St Martin-in-the-Fields,* London
188	*Projects Summary*

30 Finsbury Square

Over the last decade, compared with other European financial centres, the City of London has been successful in attracting companies involved in the financial industry. Despite Britain's refusal to join the Euro-zone, the financial district has been able to market itself as the 'innovative' player on the global scene.

left: View of Finsbury Square from the southwest corner. The two buildings to the north of the eastern block formed the site for the new building.

opposite: Perspective facade study, pencil on paper.

Unique, if not archaic market rules (e.g. Lloyd's of London, the insurance market; the London Metal Exchange, etc.) have imbued the daily working culture of the financial district with a club-like ambience, thereby further engendering interest amongst outsiders. The competitive investment in the built fabric, that is to say speculative office buildings, has been fierce, a phenomenon that has left its mark in both the Square Mile and in the seven bordering boroughs.

Finsbury Square, located just north of the City in the London Borough of Islington began as a residential development from 1777. Its atmosphere has been an amalgam of bowling green primness, standardised 1950s Festival of Britain pergolas, corporate offices set behind conservationist limestone, all conveniently supported by a lawned underground car park. Planning approval was granted to an event agency in October 2006 for the alteration to the hard and soft landscape, including the erection of a 14 m high steel arch, supporting the occasional roof protecting an 'event space'.

Eric Parry Architects office building, to the northeast of the square, positions itself as a subtle transformation of the more mechanical regularity of the neighbouring office buildings. Peter Latz, the German landscape architect had earlier been commissioned by EPA to restore the square to a more London-like, contemplative square. In an age of 'eventism', such contemplation is seen to be anachronistic; public spaces, in the minds of some planners and politicians, have to become activated, like the constant motion demanded by television.

The shaded depth of the office building's representative west facade combines a character of loftiness with the genuine massiveness of loadbearing limestone. In differentiating the tectonic tasks between peripheral piers and central cores, EPA liberate the layout while retrieving the role of the peripteral structure to stand in place of architecture.

Pier, precast lintel, reinforced concrete floor come together in a lapidary manner. Rather than the debate as to how to dress the *maison domino*, the building's tectonic conception gives rise to its physical constitution without additional dress. The exoskeletal tectonic needs no further padding or insulation, it celebrates corporeality: the pier is a pier of limestone.

And if the planners of Islington insisted that there shall be none other material than stone, then stone is what they got. 30 Finsbury Square is to modern architecture what the "maison domino" was to the derailing of modern architecture. 30 Finsbury Square, with its west and north facades, suggests that a building can consist of the things that one sees and understands, that they perform their duties in the way that they are composed, that they embody the spirit of parts to the whole in a way that the architectural profession thought no longer possible.

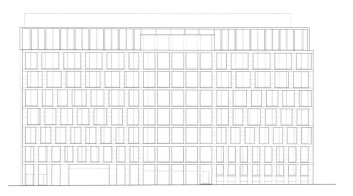

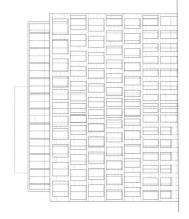

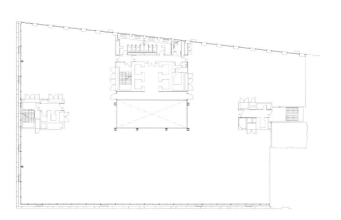

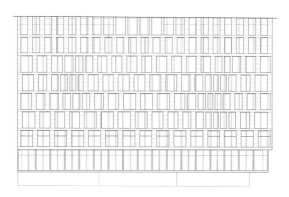

top:
Elevation to Wilson Street.

centre left:
Elevation to Christopher Street.

centre right:
Typical floor (1st–6th).

bottom:
Elevation to Finsbury Square.

If all great architecture was uninsulated, then EPA's office building is the closest thing to an uninsulated building that can be realised in a northern climate.

As to logic and discipline: EPA's design explores the logic of the cantilever, of eccentric loading, of the structural web. With the latter, the structural logic of transferring loads laterally as well as occasionally in the more conventional vertical manner, the resulting picturesque composition does a number of things: first, it both unifies the facade as well as creates a backdrop to the rest of the rather undistinguished square; secondly, the apparently haphazard pattern enlivens the configuration, which, were it to have been treated with a regular facade grid, would have been monumentally boring, given the sheer dimension of the frontage; thirdly, together with the more regular steel mullions behind, the Moiré effect of both grid systems heightens the sensation of the all too rare sense of depth in contemporary buildings, thereby effecting substance, physical presence, aura.

One branch of the theme of the picturesque in modern architecture may be traced to the designs by Dutch neo-Plasticists of the early 1920s. By way of subsequent mullion and transom window compositions as in Le Corbusier's project for a House for a Foreman of 1940 and punched openings in apparent masonry wall as in the well-known and much copied west facade of Le Corbusier's Ronchamp Chapel of 1950–1954,

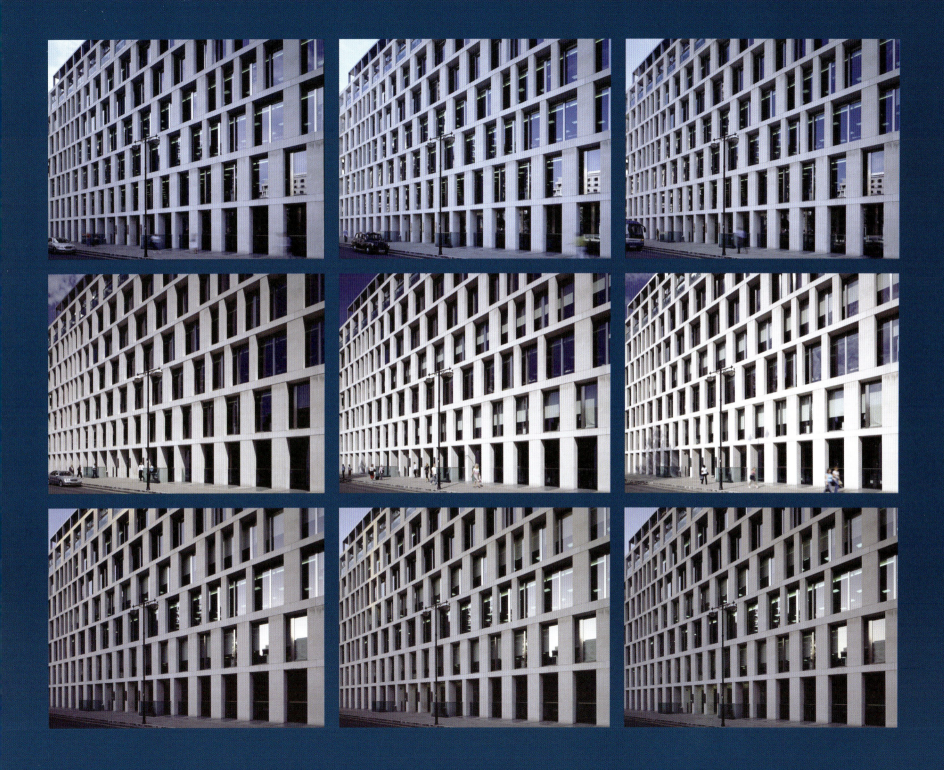

previous pages: Hélène Binet Studio's photographic study of the play of light and shadow on the stone and glass facade on Finsbury Square from dawn (top left) to dusk (bottom right).

left: The loadbearing facade of stone piers and precast concrete lintels required stacking floor on floor, reversing the norm of a swift frame erection followed by an enveloping wrap, 2001.

right: Isometric showing the assembly of elements, illustrated during manufacture and erection overleaf.

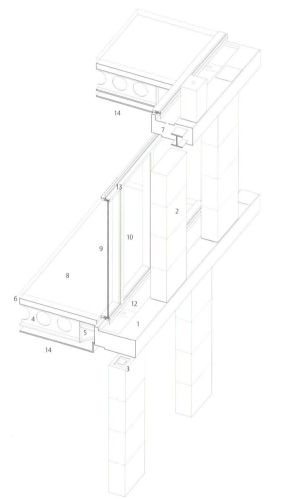

isometric

1. precast concrete beam
2. pre-tensioned Portland stone pier
3. elastomeric bearing
4. steel cell beam
5. stub beam
6. in-situ lightweight concrete slab
7. steel beam cast into pc beam
8. raised floor
9. aluminium curtain walling
10. s / s capping
11. insulation with dpm and vapour barrier
12. hopper and downpipe cast into pc beam
13. downpipe within cladding mullion
14. ceiling

left: The factory unit near the Portland quarry used by the stone contractor to assemble the finished stone blocks which were sawn and planed to achieve a tolerance of +/- 1 mm when laid on a lime mortar bed of 1000 x 400 mm. Each pier was post-tensioned by two stainless steel rods for integrity and transportation. The capacity of every block of stone had to be tested and the provenance recorded.

right: Inspection of a precast lintel. Each unit was a unique cast from a common mould, because of the irregular pier spacing. The bed of each pier had to be horizontal and stooled to stand proud of the fall of the upper face to the concealed gutter with outflows contained in the curtain wall cassettes at 6 m centres. Projecting from the back face of the lintel can be seen the steel stub to pick up the end of the 15 m long pre-cambered beams at a shear plate, see bottom left during construction.

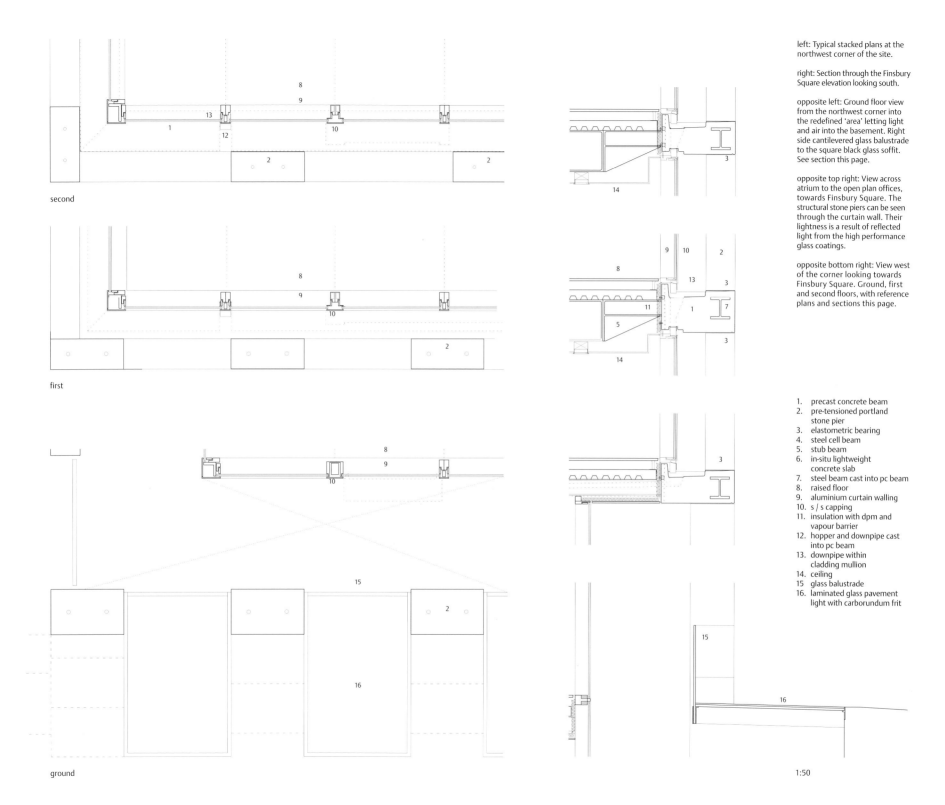

left: Typical stacked plans at the northwest corner of the site.

right: Section through the Finsbury Square elevation looking south.

opposite left: Ground floor view from the northwest corner into the redefined 'area' letting light and air into the basement. Right side cantilevered glass balustrade to the square black glass soffit. See section this page.

opposite top right: View across atrium to the open plan offices, towards Finsbury Square. The structural stone piers can be seen through the curtain wall. Their lightness is a result of reflected light from the high performance glass coatings.

opposite bottom right: View west of the corner looking towards Finsbury Square. Ground, first and second floors, with reference plans and sections this page.

1. precast concrete beam
2. pre-tensioned portland stone pier
3. elastometric bearing
4. steel cell beam
5. stub beam
6. in-situ lightweight concrete slab
7. steel beam cast into pc beam
8. raised floor
9. aluminium curtain walling
10. s / s capping
11. insulation with dpm and vapour barrier
12. hopper and downpipe cast into pc beam
13. downpipe within cladding mullion
14. ceiling
15. glass balustrade
16. laminated glass pavement light with carborundum frit

1:50

left: Inverted view in the polished stainless steel atrium bridge soffit of the glass bridge and stair at ground level.

middle: View from lower ground level of the ground level bridge and stair in the atrium.

right: View of the atrium from an office floor looking northwards. To the right the lift lobby and access bridges.

opposite: Detail of the Christopher Street elevation with the north escape stair shrouded behind the stone and precast facade.

the floodgates to unconstrained compositional freedom were opened, the effects of which are visible to this day. Many architects sense disquiet with absolutely regular facade grids, perceiving their unrelenting repetition as diminishing the significance of the configuration, depending on the relationship between the dimension of the grid to the dimension of the configuration. It is only through the accentuation of hierarchies, through the articulation of significances that the body of a volume gains in mnemonic presence. The complete enveloping of a building in a regular grid may on the other hand support the geometric unity of a volume (for example Mies van der Rohe's Seagram Building of 1954–1958), a quality that may be more desirable for freestanding objects.

In contrast to the precedent of the lower facade in Le Corbusier and Yannis Xenakis' La Tourette Monastery, 1953–1960, the piers of 30 Finsbury Square are not simply a stochastic pattern, but a carefully studied screen of local densities and opacities to achieve a remarkable balance between the senses or order and oblivious variety. The latter quality is important for the building to sustain a vitality that contrasts with the conventional effect of mechanical repetition.

Looking at the dimensions and orientation of the piers themselves, we note that there are effectively just two sets of dimensions and therefore piers and strictly speaking pillars used: the pier itself, whose short side is almost the same dimension as the sides of the pillar, a fact that helps in turning corners, whether they are at the actual external corners of the site or whether at the ground level entrance area. Here, seven piers are placed perpendicular to the facade, thereby creating further depth, an even deeper threshold.

While in the recent past, these post-neo-Plasticist, post-stochastic, post-indeterminate (John Weeks at Northwick Park Hospital, 1962–1970) notions were generally admixed into surface patterns, Eric Parry has rethought these modern traditions from their roots.

Most important to the success of the use of loadbearing stone has been the extensive research into its performance under various conditions. Tests on smaller stone samples as well as on full-scale mock-ups were undertaken to ensure that their structural and weathering performance would satisfy the necessary standards. The section through the facade then reveals the extensive honing of profiles so as to achieve the lapidary effect. Rainwater is collected in a precast rainwater recess, a secret gutter between the pier and the glazing, a detail developed at Pembroke College. This allows the facade to retain a horizontal coherence which would otherwise be heavily weathered between the piers.

The compartmental subdivision has the same direct character as the overall stance of the building: the main entrance is in the middle of the facade facing the square, from here a wide (15 m) but low lobby leads

right: View north along Wilson Street. The east facing street elevation fused the stone, concrete and framed windows into an almost flush veneer. The stable central grid seen to the left of the photograph is made up of translucent glazing to the toilets.

opposite: Hélène Binet's winter evening study of the Finsbury Square facade. The light spill at the ground floor indicates the entrance through the twisted stone piers.

to an atrium extending over the entire height. Of the nine storeys, three are special (basement with staff restaurant, entrance floor and attic), six are typical. Those parts of the building that were detailed by EPA (the usual division of labour persists in these matters, whereby an architect designs the exterior, and interior designers complete the interiors according to the various tenants' requirements, which may or may not coalesce with the 'shell') continue with slight variations on the theme of glass and steel. The atrium is treated as a reflector; the glass and stainless steel lined volume, despite its actual plan shape, enhances the sense of space.

While Eric Parry has acknowledged the formal influence of Rafael Moneo's Murcia Town Hall, 1991–1998, as a means of separating the privacy of the working environment from the civic presence of the building on the square, in the latter, the much-publicised facade towards the cathedral is a loggia. It creates an autonomous order towards the main public space while not related to the structural logic of the main volume. Thus, 30 Finsbury Square is in this sense different, if not to say a more integrated structure. From the relative autonomy of Murcia Town Hall to the corporeality of 30 Finsbury Square there is a qualitative difference.

Old Wardour House

The interstices of contemporary densely inhabited landscape attract occupants, who, by their cultivated gaze, grasp opportunities for the suitable adaptation of such gaps. The adaptation of an eighteenth century cottage besides the remnant of the late fourteenth century (Old) Wardour Castle is a recent case where a void is filled and defined by the layers of myth generated by its neighbouring architectural follies.

 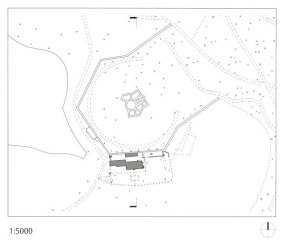

left: Watercolour view of Old Wardour Castle, 1795, of particular note is the distant tower of Fonthill Abbey designed by James Wyatt for William Beckford. It collapsed in 1825.

centre and right: Site plan and section of Old Wardour Castle and Old Wardour House. Set in a valley with spectacular views southwards the old castle was built for show rather than purely for defence. Originally moated then into an eyecatcher seen from James Paine's New Wardour Castle, 1769–1776, for the Arundell family, the old bailiff's house was built against the outer castle wall.

opposite: View from the southern valley slope an extraordinary palimpsest of life in the English country house culminating in the light-filled glass and stone extension.

Besides millennia of agriculture as the typical settlement pattern of the countryside, the construction of the ideal home is a passion pursued by a few lovers of life in the countryside. The construction of Old Wardour Castle began in 1393 on a site that was not strategically convincing. The castle was one of the first extravagant buildings in this part of Wiltshire.[1] A pleasure castle more than a defensive outpost, the building is based on a hexagonal plan with a theatrical entrance projection. The remains of the castle are surrounded by a bailey, which to the northeast opens onto a wooded area. One of the intervening owners, Sir Matthew Arundell, had Robert Smythson, architect of Longleat House, 1568–1586, visit the old castle and he may have contributed to the restoration work at the time as the architectural detail of this period suggests.

The castle was severely damaged during two Civil War sieges of 1643 and 1644, and was left a ruin, later becoming an object of contemplation from the adjoining Banqueting House (probably by James Paine, 1773–1774) while the neo-Palladian New Wardour Castle was being constructed (James Paine, 1769–1776) one and a half miles northwest of the old castle (with a chapel by John Soane of 1790).[2] A plain masonry cottage, known as Old Wardour House, was built to the south of the castle, apparently for a younger son of the Eighth Lord Arundell of Wardour, subsequently becoming the estate manager's home.

Nearby, William Beckford had commissioned James Wyatt to design Fonthill Abbey, 1795–1813, a neo-Gothic folly of gigantic proportions. One and a half centuries later, Alison and Peter Smithson constructed their minimal weekend retreat at Upper Lawn, part of the Fonthill Estate.

Luke Hughes, who inherited Old Wardour House with other family members in 1997, had known this part of Wiltshire since childhood. Given the house's location on the gentle north-facing slope, Luke and Polly Hughes decided that they wanted to introduce as much daylight into the refurbished house, which lies in a valley, as possible. The castle, which had been in the care of the state since the death of the last Lord Arundell in 1944, and its immediate surroundings had become a scheduled ancient monument and is maintained by English Heritage. Negotiations between the client, architect, the county planners and conservationists as well as English Heritage took two years; the project, constructed in large parts by Luke Hughes himself—a furniture designer by profession—took a further five years.

Originally, Old Wardour House consisted of three two-storey masonry buildings: the Main House facing south, the Summer House to the north of the inner courtyard and the former barn to the west. The three buildings had already been adapted as an extensive residence in the 1960s by Luke's mother and stepfather, but the complex remained dimly lit.

Eric Parry Architects' design for the extension of the three house complex completes what was the weakest point of the existing composition: the east facing facade of the main house, which consisted of three buttresses and a lean-to containing a service stair and toilet. Here, EPA proposed a neo-Plasticist composition of stone-enveloped wall elements containing service and storage, which in turn support a steel floor and roof slab.

The additional spaces are a large master bedroom at first floor level and the kitchen with dining area at ground level. These uses are housed in clear rectangular spaces, the projections beyond this volume reflect the articulation of the adjacent seventeenth century ruin, but more importantly, they create the multivalent impression of inhabited fragments, reused ruins, but also of a relatively simple volume that, depending on the point of view from which this addition is seen, appears both closed and transparent.

By extending and reshaping the outer two buttresses into horizontal walls (on the southern facade to the height of the parapet), the addition retrospectively 'corrects' the architectural language of the eighteenth century cottage into an abstraction of planar masonry walls with a double-pitched roof.

Similar to Finsbury Square, the addition to Old Wardour House plays with the relationship of an outer masonry screen with a recessed layer of glazing. Glass, thus shaded under certain light conditions, appears completely transparent from the outside; it is this condition that renders the addition a further fragment in the cultural landscape of ruins in and around Old Wardour Castle.

From the interior too, the external masonry structures engage the surrounding landscape of sunken stone terraces, retaining walls, old wall sections, burst bailey enclosure. The prevailing weather conditions have already absorbed the new Chillmark ashlar masonry into the continuous haptic field of patinated stonework. The stainless steel glazing elements together with the large glass surfaces thus stand more noticeably proud.

In detailing terms, the careful profiling of parapet, glazing elements and bay window (with its sliding thermal wooden screen to the south) ensure that a delicacy of detail is achieved to avoid the usual pitfall of crude singular scale that is common in much contemporary glazing. The combination of smooth stonework and heavy framing is often deadly, but here EPA show that they are fully in control of the need to differentiate and to articulate components and elements, even at the occasional risk of testing the craftsmen (and the client) to their limits.

above: Three elevations of the proposed extension, 1995. The proximity of the Grade I listed castle was a challenge. The first application which received planning permission was revised to create a simpler and cleaner contrast between solid and transparent elements.

opposite: Ground and first floor plans with roof and basement plans of the extension. The west extension was the second and longest project of a planned sequence of modifications. The summer house was converted for residential use in 1990. The new extension terminates the central passage to the west of the house.

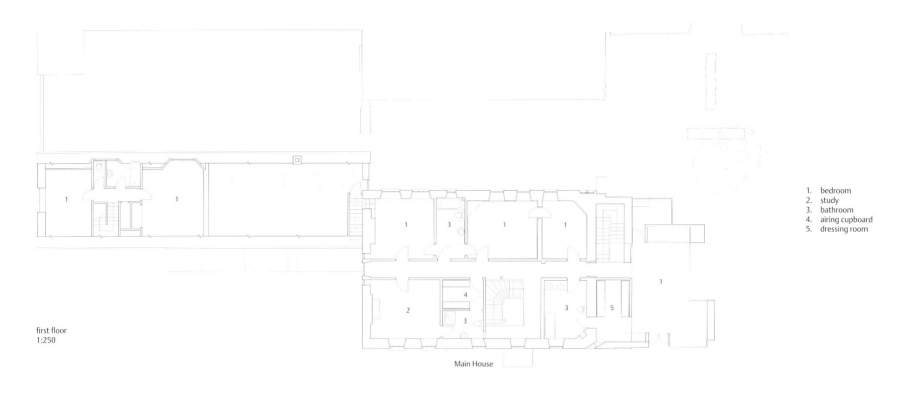

first floor
1:250

Main House

1. bedroom
2. study
3. bathroom
4. airing cupboard
5. dressing room

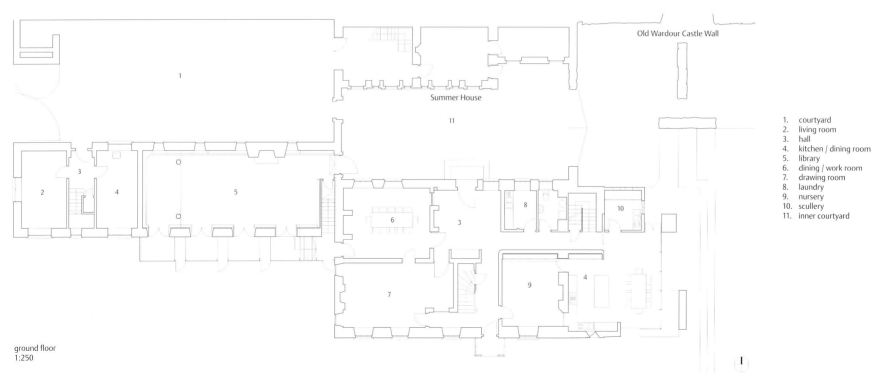

Old Wardour Castle Wall

Summer House

ground floor
1:250

1. courtyard
2. living room
3. hall
4. kitchen / dining room
5. library
6. dining / work room
7. drawing room
8. laundry
9. nursery
10. scullery
11. inner courtyard

proposed west elevation

proposed east elevation

top left: Summer house to the left, library wing to the right, entrance into the courtyard.

top right: Bedroom with large window facing ruins of a seventeenth century wing and valley beyond. Kitchen and dining space at ground floor.

middle: South elevation with the new extension to the right, unexecuted glazed passage to the library, left.

bottom: North courtyard elevation showing bedroom terrace facing Old Wardour Castle.

opposite: South elevation new stonework was stitched into the old including the old buttress. New stonework was in Chilmark to match the existing from a local quarry. The jointing and ashlar work were specified to echo examples of fine seventeenth century masonry in the garden ruins.

proposed north elevation

proposed south elevation

1:250

The design convincingly demonstrates, in this highly sensitive and charged context, how contemporary abstraction can construct an embracing multivalency that empathises with the architectural vocabulary of previous centuries while clearly and unashamedly asserting its own temporality. In this sense, there are curious parallels with the Smithson's house for themselves.

Upper Lawn Pavilion, as the Smithson's summer house is known, is a self-build two-storey addition to an existing cottage. Here, as at Old Wardour House, the interior and exterior were detailed to create a connection between new and old, giving a sense of extension and a greater scale than is actually the case. Most significantly, the sliding timber framed glazing panels could open to connect the ground floor with the surrounding garden terrace. As a freestanding building, that is to say, not in the immediate vicinity of any historic monuments, Upper Lawn Pavilion is a simpler, formally more autonomous conceit. Both Old Wardour House as well as Upper Lawn Pavilion are nevertheless, each in their own manner, manifestos of country life and of the revelation of layers as evidence of a continued respectful inhabitation of a mythological landscape.

[1] Davison, Brian K, *Old Wardour Castle*, London: English Heritage, 1999, p. 22.

[2] Caraman, Philip, *Wardour: A Short History*, Bristol, 1984, p. 17.

opposite: View from the bedroom.

ground floor

1. reconfigured eighteenth century panelled stair with access to basement
2. larder and store
3. kitchen
4. dining
5. terrace

first floor

1. stair
2. external terrace
3. dressing room
4. single glazed oriel
5. thermal sliding wall

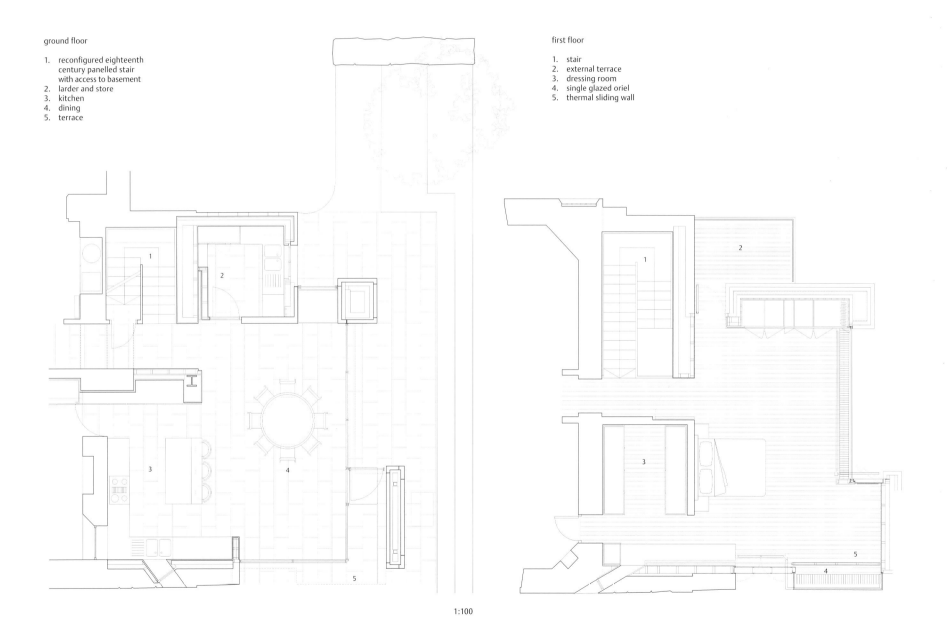

1:100

London Residence

Architects and critics working within the privileged air of qualitatively demanding designs often find it difficult to believe to which states of existence some fabrics can turn if left to the whims and fantasies of untrained eyes and minds. Visitors to London to this date are charmed much in the same way as Steen Eiler Rasmussen was all through the time he formed his ideas on London, *the unique city*.

previous page: The upright Victorian villa seen from the rear garden surrounded by a single storey curtilage which forms a terrace at first floor.

top: Evening view of the garden elevation.

bottom: House and garden on the first visit to the property, to the left an enclosed swimming pool. The interior of the house was encrusted with faux Rocaille decor.

opposite: The entrance hall, Sol LeWitt sunburst replaces the former corridor to the house stair and draws the visitor to the new enfilade of rooms to the right.

All the procurement of furniture, pictures and one-off light sculptures that grace our architecture are entirely to the credit of our collector client.

Besides the patina of centuries that covers much neglect, a uniformity in appearance remains in the memories of tourists. Georgian type terraced houses, the soot coated beige London Stock Brick, gloss painted 'stonework', the general low-rise undulation of buildings, all these things still form the overwhelming receptive frame of the city's built fabric. So much so, that anyone who can afford to own a house is so conditioned that she or he would rather own and convert an old Georgian or Victorian house than consider building something entirely new.

The strength and endurance of such a preference can be traced in journals on decoration and interiors across the post-World War II decades. The marbled mantelpiece—the hearth, despite—or because of all the invisible advantages of central heating, remains the cultural icon of this enduring preference. Educated and wealthy home searchers are first and foremost 'home buyers', buyers of ready-made homes that at the most would endure the conversion of the sanitary spaces to more abstracted and up-dated designs. The fact of owning an old house in a nation that retains one of Europe's oldest constitutional monarchies is worth considerable social kudos. Those who build anew are, on the contrary, thought of as nouveau-riche upstarts. Owning an old house, on the other hand, entertains the aura of belonging, possessing an old pile plays with the idea of one day being at least part of the wider and perhaps even narrower social establishment.

opposite: Lower terrace cut into the sloping terrain, skylight to spa below is at centre of paving. Very large glazed units face north with views onto the sunlit garden.

right: Isometric projection of extension and landscaping.

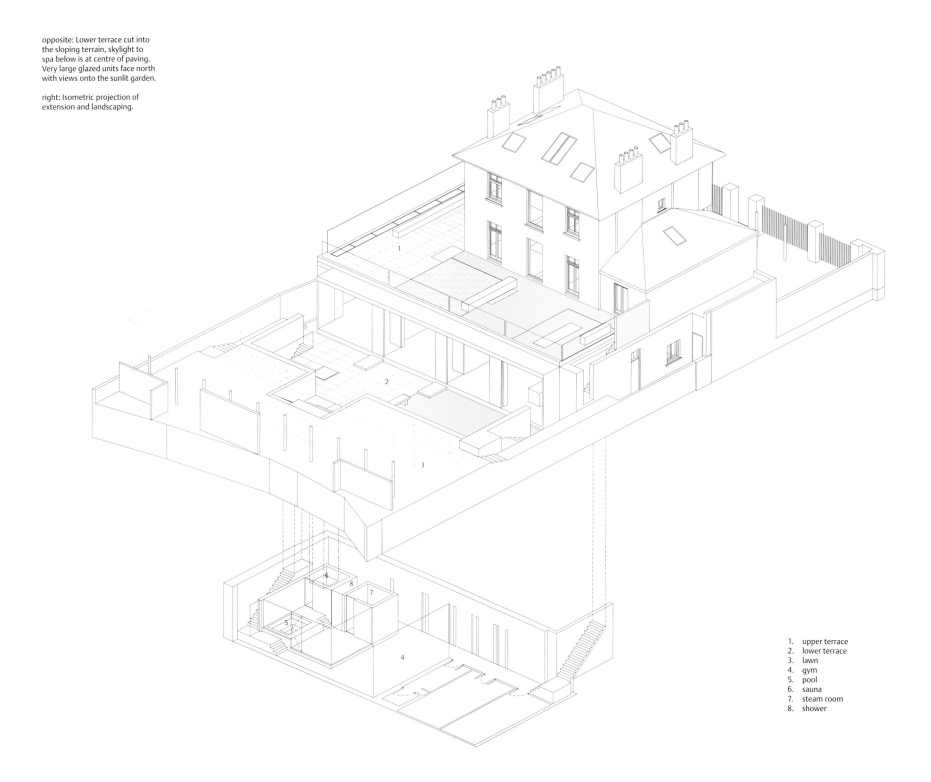

1. upper terrace
2. lower terrace
3. lawn
4. gym
5. pool
6. sauna
7. steam room
8. shower

left: Details of the stair with central glass guarding suspended from rooflight.

London is full of migrants, including from within Britain, assuming new identities, names and biographies; and if they can afford it, they want to be part of the larger social game. An entirely new house for such individuals would require more social nerve than most possess.

Besides, converting and adapting an old house is so much fun. The eager if untrained eye is thus already provided with the spatial basis upon which alteration decisions can be made. New openings, fabrics, furnishings, colours can be seen against the foil of the pre-existing building. Without a trained eye, such enthusiasm and determination often ends in the most appalling and pitiful states to which the patient and passive Georgian type house can be reduced.

The Georgian type speculative developed house forms the basis of domestic construction in Britain. Consisting of loadbearing brickwork for the external walls and wooden floors, the constructional system is patient and passive in its adaptability. Beyond its original date of birth, subsequent users and owners have no difficulty of altering all and sundries. This adaptability is both its greatest strength and weakness, as for example the images of the prior state of the St John's Wood house, which Eric Parry Architects reconfigured, show.

The street was developed as an unusually wide and tree-lined avenue with quasi-freestanding houses in the early Victorian years as an example of a more rural alternative to terraced houses. Its 'quasi' status results from the fact that ground level extensions from the main body of the house on either side have created a continuous built volume, separating generous frontcourts from the equally generously dimensioned gardens. Viewed from the street across the hedges, the dominant impression nevertheless remains one of a series of freestanding, symmetric and uniformly gloss-painted houses.

The new owners found a compilation of additions and extensions of a variety of qualities. The front facade appeared the least disjointed, the rear extension together with the lift shaft and the pool house gave an indication of the diminishing respect for both the garden as well as the architecture. The interior offered a small cabinet of horrors. All that changed with EPA's design for the house and underground spa addition, together with Christopher Bradley-Hole's landscape architectural design.

For the configurational appearance, the underlying idea was to re-establish the clarity of the freestanding early Victorian house above first floor level. Thus, apart from the northern extension containing the master bathroom and dressing room, the former configuration was retrieved. The ground floor was expanded to encompass the entire width of the site, while the pool house was removed to create a cleared sunken terrace above the underground spa. While more volume was

first floor

1. staircase
2. family room
3. master bedroom
4. master bathroom
5. dressing room
6. study 1
7. study 2
8. terrace
9. courtyard

ground floor

1. forecourt
2. entrance hall
3. living room
4. dining room
5. kitchen / breakfast room
6. garage
7. laundry
8. scullery
9. stair
10. lower terrace
11. lawn

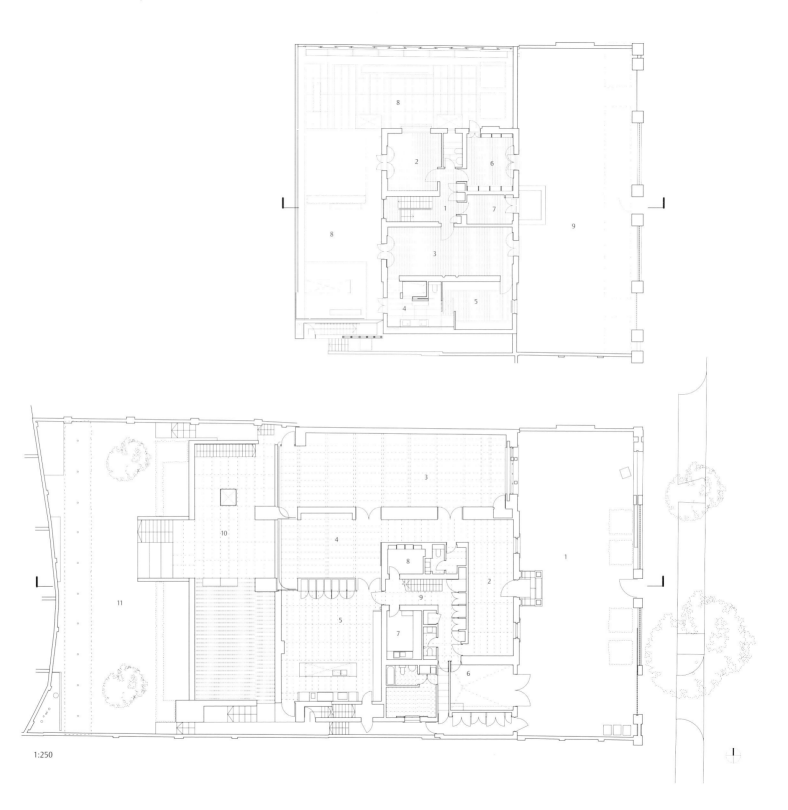

1:250

1. forecourt
2. entrance hall
3. inner hall
4. kitchen
5. lower terrace
6. lawn
7. study
8. staircase
9. upper terrace
10. bedroom
11. spa

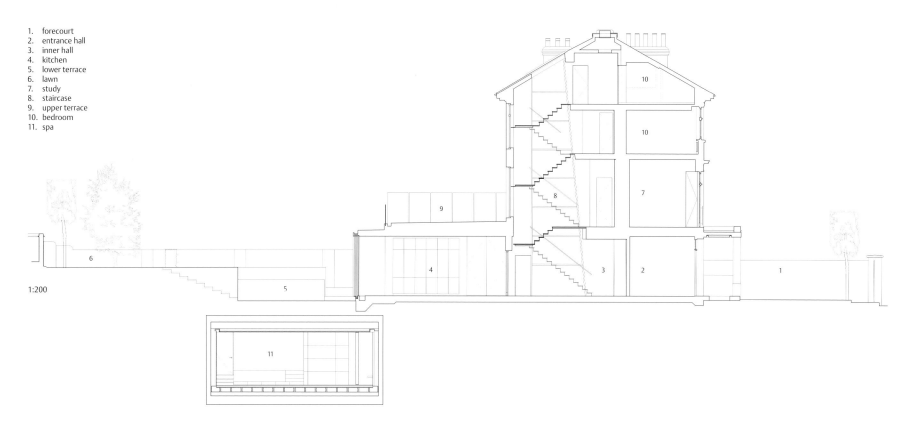

1:200

added to the site, the taut configuration with the house presented on a plinth renders the accommodated composition less obtrusive. What was once a picturesque massing of additions and extensions (diplomatically put) has now become a geometrically simpler architecture with a neo-Plasticist inspired (thus latter-day picturesque) hard and soft landscaped garden.

In terms of the architectural character, the house has now become a clearly articulated set of public and private areas. The ground floor and garden terrace are lavishly dimensioned to host receptions that can range from the highly formal to the domestic, thanks to the both the shear size of the kitchen and its vicinity to the main reception area. Rather than allowing the reception area to span the width of the site to face the garden, the kitchen almost takes centre stage. It follows the logic of the circumlocutory set of public spaces around the core of the original house, which now contains the large staircase to the private domain.

Within the lavishly proportioned spaces are contained numerous pieces of twentieth century art and furniture. The entrance hall for instance holds a Sol LeWitt mural and is perhaps the most hallowed space of the house. The reception room, while being the largest volume of the house, is furnished so as to feel like a live-in gallery. Careful indirect skylighting above to the southern party wall illuminates the art objects in this

section. The serenity of the reception/gallery is underlined by the large, dark metal doors that recall the enfilade system of mansions or palaces. Equally large panes of glass along the entire ground floor garden facade echo this sublime grandeur. EPA have used the recesses resulting from both the fitted furniture as well as from the bay-like projection of the entire ground floor garden facade to contain the luscious curtains. Within these narrow bays are contained doors to the garden terrace, thereby ensuring that the fixed glazing details can almost 'disappear'. Further, the bay-like projection of the ground floor garden facade indeed renders the 'podium' more delicate.

EPA's architectural syntax seamlessly fuses the spatial delights of Beaux Arts "poché" with the ambiguous archaic dimension of modernism. The hard landscaping extends this notion. With the sectional development from the sunken terrace to the pruned trees on the edge of the property, there is a sense of a subtle protective envelope that will slowly expand over time as the vegetation matures. There is only an inkling via the skylight of the spa below ground: here a marble clad small pool and massage area receive daylight. A steam room and sauna as well as a gym are contained in this most private of netherworlds, one that is reached via a tucked away, poché stair behind the kitchen. EPA have provided a domestic version of their earlier grand spa seen at the Mandarin Oriental in Knightsbridge.

opposite: Spa seen from the gym. Matched marble floats in the subterranean cave.

left: Morning room seen from the master bedroom, dressing rooms to the right.

opposite: Living room (distant) seen from kitchen with dining room between, which can be isolated by sliding and pivoting stainless steel screens. When closed the garden is reflected in the landscape format polished stainless steel panel seen in part.

Early Georgian aesthetics, in which Beau Brummell and the cult of bourgeois Dandyism played a large part, were pioneers of modern abstraction. Monochromatic Georgian, indeed white neo-Classical architecture (at least its latter falsified black-and-white reception) to this day provides a more tolerant option for the grafting of contemporary forms and functions. It is this open quality that allows many contemporary architects, educated in twentieth century modernism, to find a *modus vivendi* for the synthesis of Georgian architecture and the new. The glossy white houses of St John's Wood and even much of early Victorian London are a lasting proof of this aesthetic. EPA's adaptation of the villa exemplifies the necessity for a trained eye and mind so as to achieve a dignified fitness between old and new.

Royal Lancaster Hotel

Bayswater's most persistent image, despite the vicissitudes of the property market and badly managed estates, has been a glossy white painted neo-Classical development of "simply one damned house after another". Lancaster Gate and Hyde Park Gardens were planned in the mid-nineteenth century and constructed over a decade.

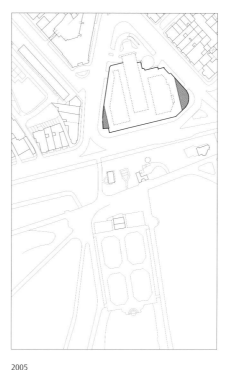

1872   1973   2005

left: The island site occupied by a dense perimeter of 40 town houses.

middle: The site cleared is reduced to a single tower and podium.

right: Heavy line indicates extent of new facade and corner infills.

The triangular space at Lancaster Gate marks the junction where the subterranean river Westbourne issued into the dammed Serpentine, the central body of water in Hyde Park. A dense accumulation of terraced houses with all the inept accoutrements of late Georgian urban design so far as the resolution of the corners in the triangular geometry is concerned covered the site.

In 1900 the narrow fronted, six-storey Park Gate Hotel opened, designed by architect Harry Bell Measures, designer of the original Central Line Stations. Located directly above the new Central Line, the hotel incorporated the street level entrance area of the underground station. The hotel was demolished in 1965 and the entire triangular block of houses was replaced in 1973 by a speculative slab and podium office, subsequently changed into a hotel.

Ever since its inception, the late modernist Royal Lancaster Hotel, an oxymoron (modern and royal) were it not for the blindness of most hoteliers and tourists to the contradictions between the aspirations of the exterior architectural expression and the faux character of its interiors, created an urban displacement by which the entire area became blighted for lack of activity and interest. The bland mindlessness of its podium formed a defensive embattlement, and the integration of the underground station on the southern facade was one of the key lessons in how not to bring together supercilious technocracy with deracinated technology. The geometry of this original podium to a large extent was aligned with Bayswater Road to the south and Lancaster Terrace to the west. The podium was set back from the northern apex of the triangular site facing Sussex Gardens in order to provide for a set down point and an anti-urban external ramp to the roof terrace car park (unfortunately this ramp and roof car park was kept, thereby precluding any sensible reconfiguration of the streetscape at this important corner). The podium's original perimeter on Westbourne Street follows the internal logic of the hotel. Seeing the structure in this light, the partial logics for the perimeter become understandable, though in the final analysis, there is neither a clear attitude towards the urban fabric, nor is there a rational idea behind the podium as an architectural object in its own right.

The owners were advised to hold a competition to add office space for the hotel administration and new meeting rooms for the existing conference facility. This followed a failed planning application. Eric Parry Architect's won the competition by showing that a reworking of the elevation could absorb this demand without raising the height of the podium. Eric Parry Architects were asked by the hotel owners, the Landmark Hotel Group, to provide a design for the complete revamping of the podium and slab's skin. So far all but the circular entrance porch of the podium has been integrated into an urban design and refaced while the hotel and underground station were functioning

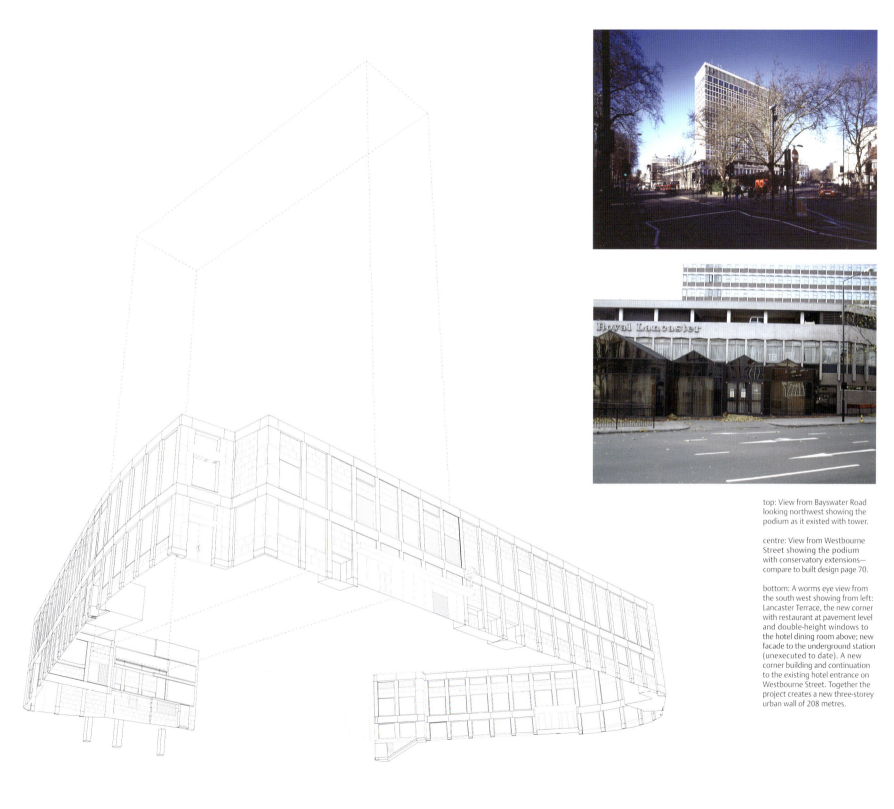

top: View from Bayswater Road looking northwest showing the podium as it existed with tower.

centre: View from Westbourne Street showing the podium with conservatory extensions—compare to built design page 70.

bottom: A worms eye view from the south west showing from left: Lancaster Terrace, the new corner with restaurant at pavement level and double-height windows to the hotel dining room above; new facade to the underground station (unexecuted to date). A new corner building and continuation to the existing hotel entrance on Westbourne Street. Together the project creates a new three-storey urban wall of 208 metres.

left: Quarry showing the generous bed dimensions necessary for the large stone elements. The stone used was a hard Spanish limestone, whiter than Portland, good for the traffic polluted island site, set against the surrounding painted stuccoed villas.

right: The construction layers from left:

1. new self-supporting stone work on a new independent concrete ground beam.
2. windows, vapour barrier and insulation.
3. existing concrete frame, with new sections at corners to Bayswater Road, stripped of precast concrete panels and modified.
4. new interior finishes to the 1.2 m building zone behind the new facade.

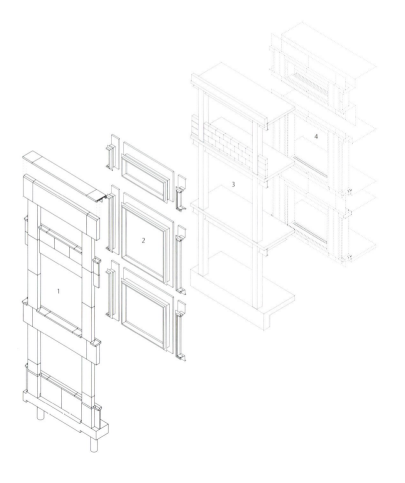

as close to normal as could be expected under these circumstances. Given the proximity to Hyde Park, the agencies concerned with the redesign included the City of Westminster, London Transport and the Royal Parks. By extending the perimeter as far as possible to the street edge, EPA have created a clearer urban figure for the podium than the previous version. To the west an entrance porch to a publicly accessible restaurant and bar almost creates a clean corner; to the east the new exterior follows the street pattern in a parallel sweep, adding a new floor of offices and meeting rooms for the existing conference facilities.

Given this urban strategy, there is an equally clear architectural approach to the new street facade. First, a horizontal datum at parapet level provides the background calm to the high-rise slab. The not insignificant change in ground level of almost six feet is stoically absorbed within the rhythmic grid of the self-supporting white limestone. Secondly, a horizontal datum at first floor level provides a *piano nobile* from which the surroundings, especially Hyde Park can be viewed. Such a strong facade grid with its pilasters and lintels allows for openings of different proportions to be contained without raising a sense of disorder. Seen from street or pavement level, the oblique or even frontal view of the facade sets off the depth required for such a sleight of hand to be effective. Thus the anomaly of the underground station entrance on Bayswater Road is absorbed within the new outer skin, as are all the ventilation louvres associated with the lift shaft and air-handling units.[1]

left: Construction section through a typical junction between the existing structure and new skin.

right: Typical bays to Bayswater Road. The granite base steps to accommodate the changes in levels across the site. Of note are the large single stone lintels up to 4 m long by 1 m high and in parts curved. The shadows are a result of careful calibration with constrained dimensions between the boundary and existing structure.

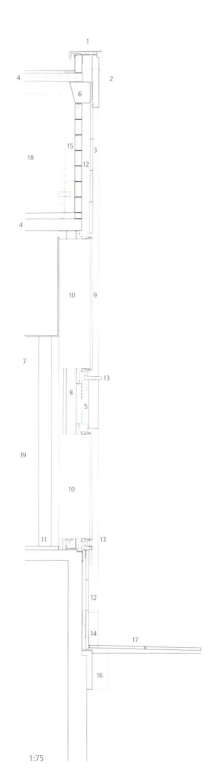

1. ppc aluminium coping
2. caliza capri limestone lintel
3. caliza capri limestone pier
4. existing concrete slab
5. insulation with dpm
6. existing concrete beam
7. ceiling
8. galvanised and painted steel curtain wall
9. mirror polished s / s window frame
10. ppc aluminium window revesl
11. ppc aluminium window cill with integrated heaters and lighting
12. caliza capri limestone ashlar panel
13. caliza capri limestone cill
14. granite plinthstone with weap holes
15. blockwork with dpm
16. reinforced concrete footing
17. pavement
18. carpark
19. Nine Kings Ballroom

1:75

opposite: View from Bayswater Road. The new corner incorporates the hotel offices as an additional floor within the existing podium height.

top: View westwards along Bayswater Road. A section of the old facade is visible around the tube entrance. It represents the failure of entangled bureaucracy.

bottom: View of new corner building to Lancaster Terrace.

Further, so as to demonstrate the factuality of the stonework as a massive construction, EPA included a semi-hewn lintel in the grand window above the entrance to the restaurant and a rough-hewn panel on the blank wall adjacent to this entrance. The lintel's simultaneous polished vertical face and its rough underbelly, as well as the segment of rough-hewn stone give evidence of the stone's original state, analogous to Claude Lévi-Strauss' notions of "the raw and the cooked": extreme conditions from nature to culture.

However, in these earlier Structuralist metaphors, the notion of nature was itself mythologised. Nature, now being in an endangered state, is no longer 'the raw', but increasingly an ideal state whose status is considered higher than the 'cooked'. By implication, the self-loadbearing masonry is only marginally more 'cooked' than the rough-hewn blocks in the contemporary context of representational tectonics.

While the self-supporting masonry of the new podium to the Royal Lancaster Hotel appears both in colour as in constructional behaviour to resemble the tradition of classical orders as seen in the high-Victorian houses of the Lancaster Gate and Hyde Park Gardens estates, it is to this representative tectonics as Protestantism is to Catholicism. Similarly, the self-supporting masonry is to the late modern curtain wall of the slab as fundamentalism is to pragmatism. On the one hand, EPA's efforts could be regarded as a rearguard action, completely out

left: Door handles in wood and polished stainless steel to the island restaurant.

right: Handrail detail and coloured stucco at the junction of an existing fire escape lobby and the new skin.

opposite: View of the building's openings at dusk.

of date, pointless. On the other hand, the simple pristine materiality is so fundamentally different and basic that the newly enveloped podium has become the touchstone of the corporeality previously discussed. The porosity of the Spanish limestone is simply and utterly different to the glossy seal provided by the innumerable coats of external paint that have indiscriminately been slopped over the stuccoed surfaces of the late-Victorian houses. The limestone echoes another era, maybe one that is not ours, where things are once again closer to what they seem.

The effort taken in the detail of the self-supporting masonry is matched by that of the glazing details. The new windows consist of very large frames inserted into the newly formed masonry openings. Besides the fact that their profiles are honed such that the sharpness of the frame, the flatness of the glass, become supportive of the tectonic reading of the masonry, they possess a lightness quite uncharacteristic of standard industrial profiles. It is this seeming effortlessness, the matt quality of the stone, the insistence on the quality of the opening as an opening, the palpableness of the supported loads that is taken for granted in an era in which only a technological feat or an outrageous event register. One hopes the owners of the hotel can find the commitment to continue with the renovation of the tower and more significantly the commitment to create an integral design of the intensity of the self-loadbearing facade of the podium.

[1] The works to this section of the facade are yet to be carried out.

*The London
Stock Exchange*

Few sites in urban culture have such a dense and chequered history as the precinct surrounding St Paul's Cathedral. A subject of national debate, the redevelopment of one of the largest coherent pieces of property in central London, at the historic heart of the financial district, became the battleground of urban design ideas and architectural languages.

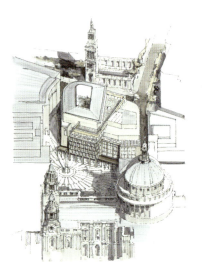 

left and right: Presented with a trapezoidal site bisected by differential height constraints and by the masterplanner's vision of a monumental loggia to the new Paternoster Square, these early sketches were an attempt to suggest an alternative to the loggia form proposed (stone columns supporting brick vaults).

opposite: Sketch elevation to Newgate Street, showing the stone shell, five storeys to the east and six to the west, intersected by the more crystalline upper levels along the St Paul's height fault line. The articulation of the stone piers at 6 m centres echoes the pragmatic nineteenth century London warehouse elevation. The precast concrete horizontal lintels are supported by the stone piers.

If it is true that World War II was a logical consequence of the mechanisation and technocratisation of modern society, then the debates about the correct scale of urban and architectural development on such a large site produced a variety of knee-jerk reactions. A coherent, homogeneous realisation of a Le Corbusian plan quasi *à redants*, William Holford's 1956 design conformed to the current ideal of a homogenous architectural entity designed by one architect, regardless of its dimensions.[1] The development, 1961–1967, was an anti-urban block structure, an insertion of a large alien figure, as alien as many then contemporary structures that found their way into the still tightly knit urban fabric, but no longer densely populated City (population of the City of London in 1900: 26,923, in 2005 (estimated) 9,185).

At the height of popular postmodernism, and it is worth remembering that this stylistic movement was abetted in London first by academia and then by the mass-media followed by the quaint but nevertheless determined efforts of a member of the royal household, Holford's Paternoster Square complex became the *bête noire* of all those who had mustered enough courage to speak out against bad modern architecture, of which there was and still is a lot in London.

Part of this vitriolic reaction towards Holford's Paternoster Square complex were the helter-skelter, but ultimately botched attempts over the course of a decade from 1986 to 1995 at finding a suitable masterplanner as well as the self-appointment of an architect, who had the explicit blessing of Prince Charles, to propose an alternative masterplan in the realistic mode of Disney, in effect a classical megastructure to replace the modernist one. For all participants, the new Paternoster Square was to be a departure from the normal commercial cannibalisation of an already anaemic inner city fabric. However, without the inclusion of any residential use, Paternoster Square could only ever become another instance of functional zoning reserved for the financial industry with architecture forced to compensate for the absence of any active urban culture. After six o'clock in the evening, the City of London was like a vacated film set, ideal for urban archaeologists who like a bit of quiet.

The legitimacy in speaking of knee-jerk reactions towards Holford's Paternoster Square is provided by the inconsistent reception of modern architecture in Britain. Thus, the Barbican Estate by the architects Chamberlin, Powell and Bon, 1965–1976, built for the Corporation of the City of London, is considered by numerous commentators as a significant landmark.[2] Yet in reality, it is a more extreme, anti-urbanist intervention on an even larger scale than Holford's Paternoster Square. Perhaps it was the soft landscaping that successfully ameliorated the Barbican's monumental monotony; its convoluted circulation is probably not even matched by that of the South Bank Arts Centre, south of the Thames.

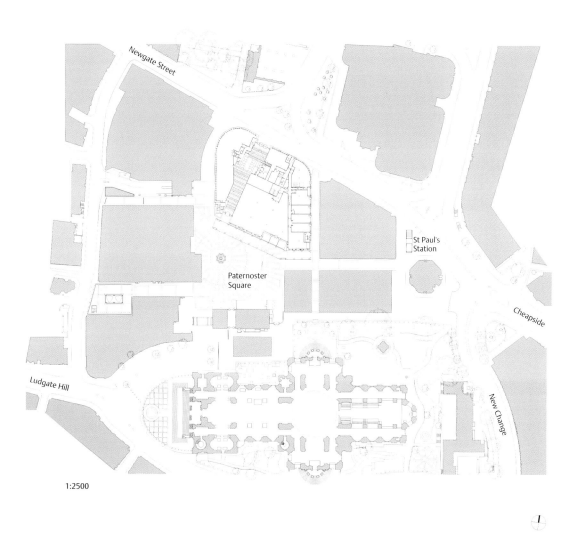

1:2500

Site plan of Paternoster Square defined by the office buildings developed within the William Whitfield masterplan.

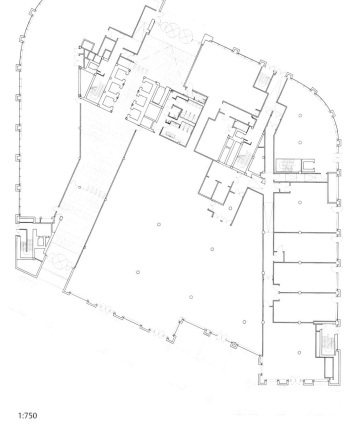

1:750

Ground floor. The building is bounded to the south by the Whitfield loggia, to the north by Newgate Street and to the east and west by two passages. Retail use to the east of the central passage connects the north and south entrances.

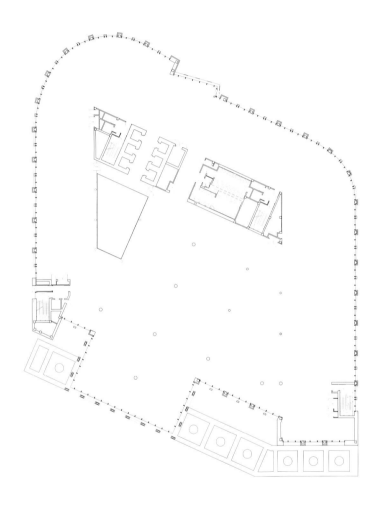

First floor. In order to accommodate a trading floor if required this floor was designed with a larger sectional dimension. This allowed the LSE to house both TV facilities and an auditorium.

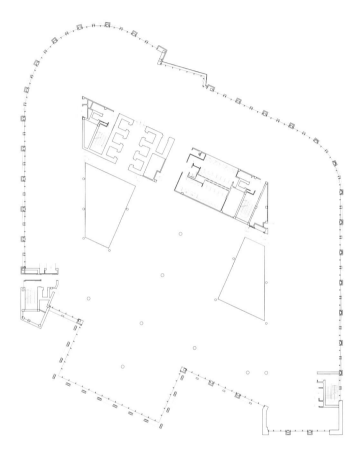

Typical floor—second to fifth floors. The twin atriums draw natural light into a plan depth of 60 m in both the north–south and east–west axes.

Construction photograph from St Paul's dome dated September 2002 illustrating the formidably congested site. Temporary site huts occupied the square itself and access to the site was limited to the passages from Newgate Street and the subterranean service route.

Holford's Paternoster Square was the victim of neglect by its leaseholders. Poor marketing left large sections of the development unused. As a result, the design managed to attract the scathing criticism of the growing postmodernist adherents in the mid-1980s. Paternoster Square was like a lightning conductor that protected all the other monstrosities from equally abrasive strikes such as the adjacent British Telecom City headquarters or the 'Noddy' office block opposite the Museum of London.

The original owners of the Paternoster Square site, the Church Commissioners, had sold long leases to the Central Electricity Generating Board (CEGB) and the contractors, who had built the Holford scheme in 1967. From this date to the completion of the final design, leasehold ownership changed five times; the current leasehold owner—Mitsubishi Estate Co. Ltd.—could theoretically remain in possession of the development until the year 2236. Altogether four masterplanners were appointed by the various leaseholders from 1987 to 1996, and a total of 23 architectural practices were intensively involved, both as masterplanners as well as architects for individual buildings. Besides the Church Commissioners (represented by the Surveyor of St Paul's, Sir William Whitfield, in the end the last masterplanner), the Corporation of the City of London, the Commission for Architecture and the Built Environment (CABE), the Royal Fine Art Commission, English Heritage, a wide cast of developers, property consultants and contractors, not to mention pressure groups from the architectural journalists to the unofficial go-betweens, the task of masterplanning such a loaded site was unenviable.

In the final analysis, William Whitfield's realised masterplan can be regarded as a culmination of a line of thought that was shared by Skidmore, Owings and Merrill and Stirling Wilford & Associates' competition entries of 1987–1988, which in turn were followed by Farrell, Simpson and Beeby's joint masterplans of 1991 and 1993. The scale of buildings to replace Holford's snaking extrusions were of the same magnitude in these five schemes, all of which were significantly larger than the fine grain of the post-Great Fire of London fabric. Effectively, what used to be urban blocks with dozens of parcels were replaced by single buildings. Following the wholesale destruction brought on by the German Luftwaffe during World War II, and the subsequent demolition of Holford's complex, the new Paternoster Square found its literary promoter in Peter Ackroyd, for whom "the shape of the old territory is being revived. It is as if London were some organic being with an underlying form of its own, a form that emerges even after the most catastrophic circumstances."[3]

Undoubtedly, the new Paternoster Square development for Mitsubishi Estate is a smaller grained complex. It is thankfully all grounded at street level. Of course one could argue that, even without taking the realised architecture into account, the new scale conforms more

left and right: An innovative gantry system to both east and west elevations was developed to allow many teams of stonemasons to work on the hand set stone and precast wall simultaneously. A continuous platform 90 m long was lifted in one piece to follow the progress of the work.

closely to the image of the City of London; that is to say, the image that it would like to project of itself. Yet it is precisely this image that has little to do with the reality of the financial district. The clear trajectory for the City of London is to slowly but unrelentingly replace every single building, perhaps not their entire facades, but at least all of their inner workings, while being hamstrung by the image of a Medieval street pattern and at least a Victorian streetscape. This is the way some 80 per cent of the fabric in the City of London has already been 'renewed' since World War II.[4]

Part of this mythologised image is the narrowness of the alleys; some of the most successful urban moments are the visually controlled views, particularly of St Paul's Cathedral. Less successful is the suspended domed colonnade that Whitfield designed and which Eric Parry Architects and MacCormac Jamieson Pritchard had to integrate into their buildings. It would have been more intelligent had the masterplanner relinquished control over its actual design and merely insisted on its typology.

With regard to 10 Paternoster Square itself, the largest building amongst the complex, it was conceived as a speculative office with the usual requirement for the possibility of subdivision, multiple entrances, a range of internal spaces (from individual to group offices, as well as the usual set of communal facilities). Whitfield's 1997 masterplan defined a footprint which EPA took on board virtually unchanged, save

top: North elevation to Newgate Street, western lanterns of the Cathedral shown behind.

bottom: West elevation to Rose Street, the rhythm of the 6 m centred stone piers from the Newgate Street corner terminate in the solid stone walls of the southern core facing Paternoster Square.

north elevation Newgate Street

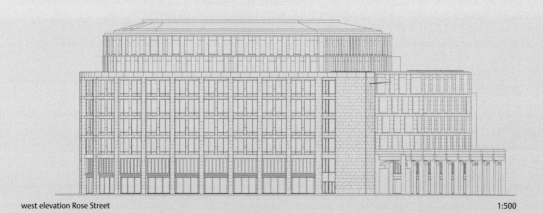

west elevation Rose Street

1:500

three details: the two radiused corners on Newgate Street and the pavilionisation of the central volume, as if it were a miniature tower on a rather high podium. Given the commercial pressure to maximise net floor area and the additional configurational constraints, including the St Paul's Cathedral sight line regulations, EPA amassed two storeys at attic levels to the building's west, where the main vertical core had been located.

Thus the typical floor plan consists of essentially a perimeter of double and single loaded offices, with special spaces containable either at the core or at the southwestern projecting wing of the pavilion. Rather than Whitfield's footprint, which employed certain corner treatments that required specific grid dimensions for their regular resolution, EPA's use of radiused corners, coupled with the off-axis opening set-back of the attic glazing system, allows a collage of three configurational systems: the masonry bay, the attic glazing system and the implied presence of the orthogonal pavilion even on Newgate Street. It is as if the geometrically adjusted compositional principles established at Bedford's Music School with its almost autonomous temple-like recital hall and its brick enveloped practice and teaching wings were once again being applied at 10 Paternoster Square. Here three tectonic systems echo those of the Music School: stone cladding to the pavilion to the steel panels at the recital hall, masonry bays to brickwork, large-scale glazing as cohesive elements.

The configuration of 10 Paternoster Square is effective: the whole building twists and adjusts to the non-orthogonal site allowing the different configurational components to perform their relatively autonomous architectural role. It would have been an easy matter for EPA to have adopted and adapted the Whitfield colonnade as a fourth configurational element so as to have resolved the relationship between loggias and bays, if it had only been permitted. Then the colonnade would have become the palpable corporeal tectonic to an assembly of self-loadbearing piers, not a hundred miles away from the concept behind 30 Finsbury Square. Archetypically, the tripartite composition of pavilion, flash-gaps and lateral wings, as seen on the southern side, conforms to the classical language of palazzi and Venetian villas. The fact that the main entrance from the new square is not located within the pavilion frontage suggests that pragmatic considerations overrode archetypal conventions.

With regard to the facade detailing, essentially two types can be identified: the screen and the bay. The non-loadbearing masonry, formally related to 30 Finsbury Square, though in constructional terms more conventional, and the matted glass panels (as part of a double curtain wall system) represent the screen; their identical picturesque manner of composition confirms their kinship. The 6 m bay with its partially self-loadbearing masonry is more of a conventional cladding system than the new facade to the Royal Lancaster Hotel. The tectonic language expresses this: the pillars are more literal; the concrete backed crowning 'lintel' is more abstracted. Therefore, from the tectonic composition to the configuration, 10 Paternoster Square is a hybrid of 30 Finsbury Square and the new podium to the Royal Lancaster Hotel are the gauging poles.

In this key location, it is unsurprising that the London Stock Exchange, itself a listed company acting as a market maker, would rent part of the building. The Exchange had been looking for new premises which better reflected and accommodated their more open organisational requirements which their previous high-rise building on Threadneedle Street could not offer. The building offers photo opportunities from both inside as well as outside. Television studios have been installed on the first floor to take such advantage.

It has unfortunately become common practice amongst previously authoritative institutions, such as a nation's stock exchange, for these no longer to be their own clients. The history of stock exchange buildings in London is a long one, but one that ended in the 1960s in Threadneedle Street. While EPA, the leaseholders Mitsubishi Estate and their letting agents can feel pride at having such a distinguished tenant, the fact that the Stock Exchange did not commission their own building is another indication of the fundamental change in culture in Western societies that deeply affect architecture. While at least in London, the market managers have decided to stay within the ceremonial county of the City of London, the German stock exchange, for example, moved from Frankfurt's inner city to a location on the dull periphery in Hausen, not even in suburbia. The age of spaceless trading has killed off the traditional trading floor and opened the door to decentralised and remote screen control from any location: atopia.

Where markets once were physical entities giving birth to dense settlements that later became known as towns and cities, contemporary trading systems systematically deny or undermine the necessity for such settlement structures. London, Frankfurt and other cities are merely clutching on to their historic market making institutions for as

left: The noon-dial was another collaboration with dialist Dr Frank King and the letter designer and cutter Lida Cardozo-Kindersley (see also the Pembroke sundial EPA Volume 1). The optimised structure of the 5.5 m cantilever to hold the gnomon disk which casts a spot of light passing over the equation of time cut into the stone wall was developed by optimised structures engineer Dr Kristina Shea.

right: View between the Chapter House and new offices from the north wall of St Paul's Cathedral.

opposite: View of the building from the relocated (2004) Temple Bar designed by Christopher Wren 1672. The massing of the fragmented southern elevation allows the relatively small public space to breathe. If pure commerce had had its way this wall would have been a continuous eight storeys. Sir William Whitfield the masterplanner designed the anachronistic loggia, hard landscaping and central monument.

long as they can. In view of the already aggressively pursued 'consolidation' of stock exchanges around the world, the reduction in stock exchange market makers is inevitable. Their rental of non-commissioned speculative offices is an early indicator of their spatial dissolution. Those who do not build for themselves are not here to stay. Diplomatically put, EPA's design for 10 Paternoster Square, as for the Paternoster Square development on the whole, can be regarded as indexes of a looser fit between users and buildings. Compared to even twentieth century urban culture, it becomes clear that the new Paternoster Square development mimics urban life, highlighting the way in which London as a whole has radically changed.

[1] Mumford, Lewis, *Technics and Civilisation*, New York, 1934, pp. 309–311; "For war is the supreme drama of a completely mechanised society; ... Thus war breaks the tedium of a mechanised society and relieves it from the pettiness and prudence of its daily efforts, by concentrating to their last degree both the mechanisation of the means of production and the countering vigour of desperate vital outbursts. War sanctions the utmost exhibition of the primitive at the same time that it deifies the mechanical. In modern war, the raw primitive and the clockwork mechanical are one.... as long as the machine remains an absolute, war will represent for this society the sum of its values and compensations: for war brings people back to earth, makes them face battle with the elements, unleashes the brute forces of their own nature.... This destructive union of the mechanised and the savage primitive is the alternative to a mature, humanised culture capable of directing the machine to the enhancement of communal and personal life. If our life were an organic whole this split and this perversion would not be possible, for the order we have embodied in machines would be more completely exemplified in our personal life, and the primitive impulses, which we have diverted or repressed by excessive preoccupation with mechanical devices, would have natural outlets in their appropriate cultural forms. Until we begin to achieve this culture, however, war will probably remain the constant shadow of the machine: the wars of national armies, the wars of gangs, the wars of classes: beneath all, the incessant preparation by drill and propaganda towards these wars. A society that has lost its life values will tend to make a religion of death and build up a cult around its worship—a religion not less grateful because it satisfies the mounting number of paranoiacs and sadists such a disrupted society necessarily produces."

This text, originally written in 1931, foresaw the developments of the subsequent decades, including those of the early decade of the twenty-first century.

[2] Ironically, in the various stages of design, the early versions for the Barbican included a Holfordian Paternoster Square; see the model view in *Rebuilding Cities* by Percy Johnson-Marshall, Chicago, 1966, ill. 109 on p. 266.

[3] Ackroyd, Peter, "Introduction", *The Story of Paternoster: A new Square for London*, ed. Nicola Jackson, London, 2003, p. 4.

[4] Wang, Wilfried, "The City of London, Camden and the Isle of Dogs", *Tradición y Cambio en la Arquitectura de seis Ciudades Europeas*, Madrid, 1992, pp. 55–76.

Bedford Library

The complexities of realising contemporary architecture in the context of large institutions, whose self-understanding should never be underestimated, cannot be adequately summarised. If an architect's work for a long-standing friend can sometimes be a test of patience, the struggles with a corporation and a planning authority following the successful outcome of a competition process separates the men from the boys.

The radiused corner, inflected facade and window into the ground floor are an invitation to the liberation of the knowledge the inside offers. The horizontality of the library is in contrast to the institutional rectitude of the Victorian main school building, a commentary on the individual and the collective.

Site plan showing location of the new library and music school on sites seen between the framework of other buildings and reinforcing the character of each setting.

1. library, 2004
2. music school, 2006
3. main school building, 1891, reconfigured, 1979
4. playing fields
5. chapel

1:5000

Eric Parry Architects have mastered previous encounters with representatives of established institutions, and the positive working atmosphere with the authorities of Bedford School clearly carried over to the subsequent project of the new Music School on the other side of the enormous sports field with six cricket pitches.

Bedford School, though amongst the oldest public schools in Britain, was relocated to its present somewhat reclusive site on the interior of an enormous suburban block in the northern part of the eponymous town in 1891.[1] Its architecture consists most notably of a dominant Victorian Great Hall (reconstructed following an arson attack in 1979 in a mixture of late Victorian Gothic on the north facade facing the sports field and a more repetitive institutional character on the south facade), an early twentieth century stripped Arts and Crafts Chapel and a series of uninspiring twentieth century boxes. In an effort to improve the quality of its built fabric, the school held a limited design competition in 2000 for a new library building on a site adjacent to the inadequate library building of 1920.

EPA won the competition with their proposal for a brick-clad building that opens towards the west with two gables and looks across to the playing fields via a glazed ground floor corner opening to the north and east. In its configuration, the library almost exactly mediates between the alignment of the suburban houses to the north of the site and the disposition of both Memorial Hall and Great Hall to the east. The resulting change in angle is expressed in the concave facade towards the old, two-storey Memorial Hall. The south facade of the shorter wing of the new library meets the southern facade of Memorial Hall. These salient qualities circumscribe the degree of fitness between the new building and its heterogeneous context. Rather than treating the library as a singular volume, the creation of an asymmetric U with a major and minor wing echoes the backs of the suburban houses, yet towards the school proper, the tall brickwork at first floor level provides a monumental scale capable of taking measure with the eastern neighbours.

The separation of the ground floor from the upper level is expressed in a material change—rendered concrete blockwork painted the same light grey colour as the reinforced concrete columns, and originally conceived as precast concrete panels, versus the uniform—allows the building to appear lighter, a characteristic that is abandoned on the western side, where the two levels of windows directly beneath the vaulted roof create their own sense of large scale.

ground floor

1. entrance lobby
2. librarian
2a. office
3. catalogue reference and bag store
4. library garden
5. library
6. periodicals and newspapers

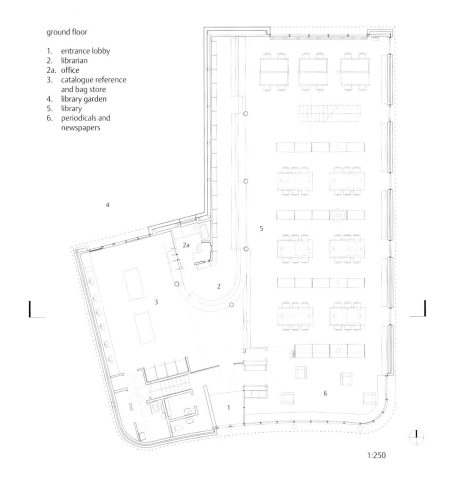

first floor

1. library upper level
2. seminar room
3. lightwell with north light
4. rooflight over

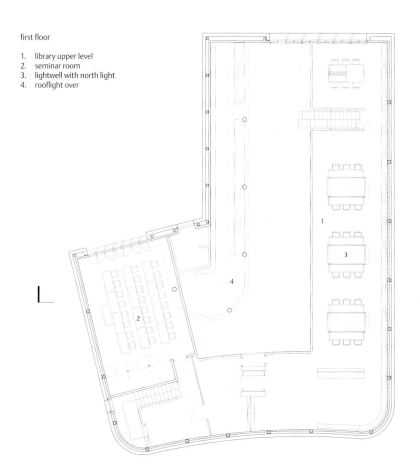

1:250

Cutaway perspective showing the steel barrel vaulted roof structure with its complex geometry. The first floor wall is a full brick thick and wraps 56 m around the building without a movement joint.

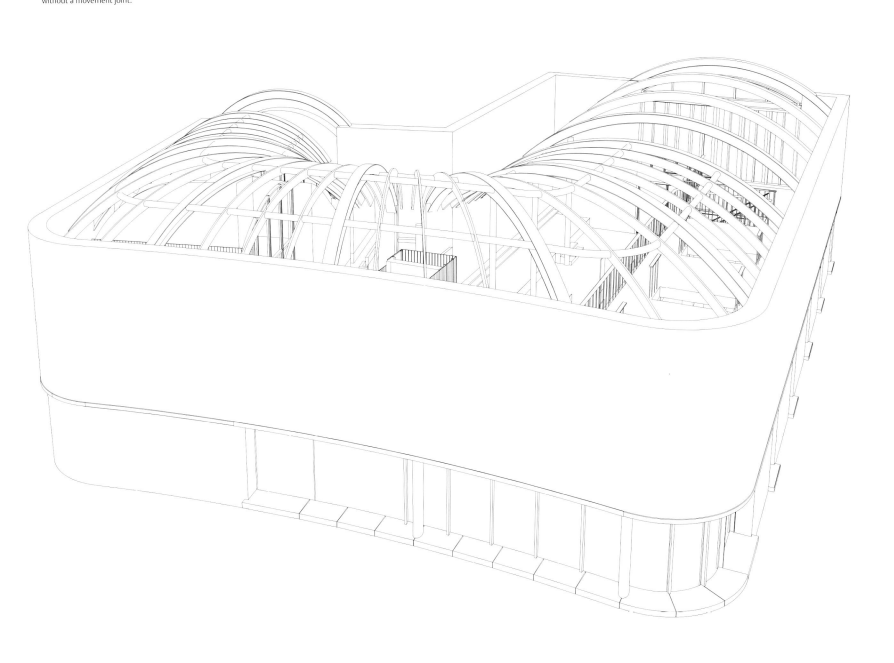

Elevations.
The building was carefully designed and orientated to minimise solar gain whilst optimising natural daylight.

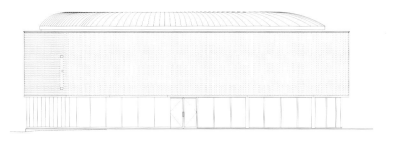

east elevation

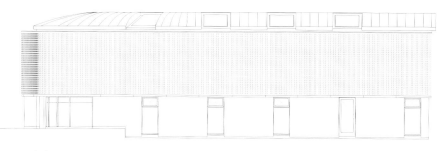

north elevation

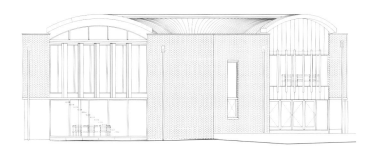

west elevation

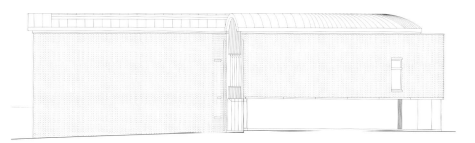

south elevation

1:250

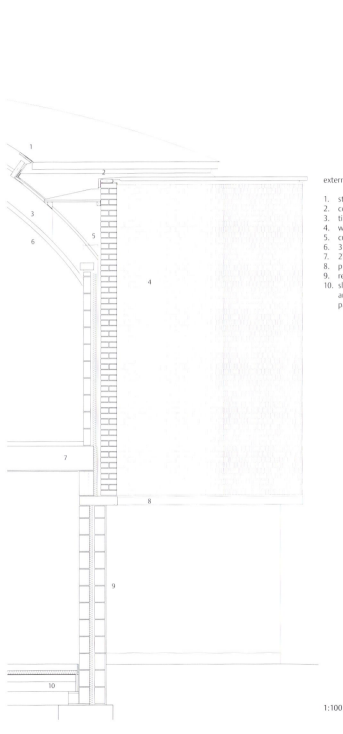

external wall section

1. standing seam pre-weathered
2. coping and gutter
3. timber joist
4. wirecut facing brick
5. curved u.b and wind posts
6. 3 coat plaster on metal lathe
7. 275 mm concrete slab
8. precast concrete ledge lintel
9. render
10. slab with underfloor heating and reclaimed hardwood parquet flooring

1:100

In the interior, the two wings are understood much more as belonging to one U-shaped volume, a sense that is created by the vaulted ceiling, even though the radii of the two roof sections differ significantly and palpably, and the peripheral gallery in the shorter wing, turns into a multi-purpose or exhibition space. The combined primary curved steel I-sections and secondary curved laminated timber sections form the rigid roof structure, which as a result of inbedded wind posts and the thickness of the wall construction, does not need any tie rods.

Following the efficient library type by Alvar Aalto, in which a single person at a central control desk is able to overlook all significant spaces, the inside of the U, so to speak, becomes the ideal site for the librarian on duty. Were it not for the enclosure to the multi-purpose room, the short section would be both a *répétition différente* of Ètienne-Louis Boullée's Bibliothèque Nationale (project of 1785) and in its wake Henri Labrouste's Bibliothèque St-Geneviève, 1843–1851, in Paris, in which the notion of the visibility and palpability of the entirety of human knowledge is translated into a terracing of bookcases and galleries forming the obverse of a giant vaulted space, itself a symbol of unity and completeness. Labrouste's central cast iron colonnade of the Bibliothéque St-Geneviève, the galleried reading spaces, the lofty vaulting are reiterated here for an ambitious public school, finally eager to create a legacy also in its architecture.

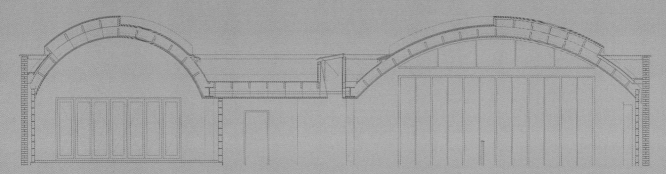

1:100

If some of the details look heavy—the rainwater hoppers, the profiling of the roof edge above the double-height windows on the end elevations, the homogeneity of the Flemish bond brickwork (in contrast with the variegated colours of Memorial Hall, for instance, which create depth)—the vast majority of design decisions are refined and even riskily delicate (considering the amount of wear and tear at a school). The balustrade at gallery level, for instance, succeeds in remaining light. The reading tables and the built-in seating at ground level are of a minimal succinctness that will ensure their longevity. Therefore, while the exterior asserts an institutional authority, the interior offers a distinct sense of relief, almost an atmosphere of informality that appears to be highly welcomed by the pupils.

A key role in this dual character is played by the double-height window on the west facades: the form with its arched top could be argued to allude to the neo-Gothic windows of the Great Hall while also creating depth by using a splayed *brise-soleil* of prefabricated concrete. Together with the wooden window frames, these details play with different scales of perception. EPA's effort at this complex perception can be recognised; it shows, alas, a most unusual intensity and commitment to determining the nature and shape of every component of the built fabric.

The brickwork is of Ketley engineering class B grade and in this context shows equal resolution: 'special' radiused stretcher determined the radii of the rounded corners. Most importantly, in order to avoid movement joints in the 56 metres of continuous wall, hydraulic lime mortar was tested and used. While in the long term the wall should remain free of cracks, the construction programme for the brickwork was exceeded. The lime mortar was unfortunately adversely effected by the freeze-thaw cycle, thereby giving rise to mortar staining on the external brick surface for a few seasons. Although this was not intended by the architects, the residue has created a patination that relieves the overbearing homogeneity of the continuous brick surface.

The reinforced concrete components (columns and the brick supporting precast toe) are all protected by a colourless sealant (Keim Lotexan-N). Given the need to thermally insulate the building, these elements are thus the only ones that remain nakedly massive and unencumbered by insulation. They are therefore the sole instances of true corporeality, even though the extensive and visually dominant Flemish bonded brick wall aspires to this quality. Having said this, an argument could be made to suggest that the entire configuration in its flowing uninterrupted vault and the plasticity of the brickwork would lay claim to this quality.

[1] Bedford School is a public school for boys, refounded in 1548, royal patent of 1552. It is making a considerable effort at attracting pupils whose parents are unable to afford the average annual fees of between £8500 (day boys) and £20700 (boarders). The school is part of a network of 4 schools run by the Harpur Trust, a charity established in 1566 by Sir William Harpur (endowment valued at £58.2 million in 2006).

left: Section A–A. The minimised excavation responds to volumes and allows the librarian a controlling view of library spaces.

right: Evening view from the library garden through the west gate to the library interior.

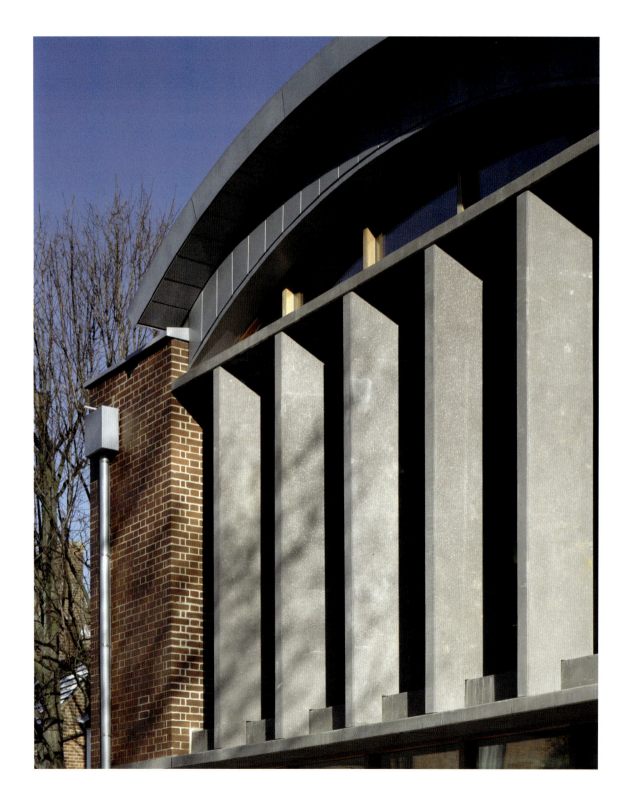

left: Precast fins to upper level of the west gable provide shading.

opposite: View to west end and upper level of the reading room. Bespoke butterfly uplighters wash the barrel vault at night.

Bedford Music School

The new Music School is sited next to the school's Chapel, enjoying a privileged and direct view across the central playing fields, The Chapel is the other spiritual centre of the public school tradition. The siting of the Great Hall and Chapel reinforce each other's status, and thus it is no surprise that such a relationship is sought by any additional building that over the course of time will reshape the closest thing to a *forum anglicanum*, even at the expense of relinquishing a few square feet of that much valued, if amorphous playing field.

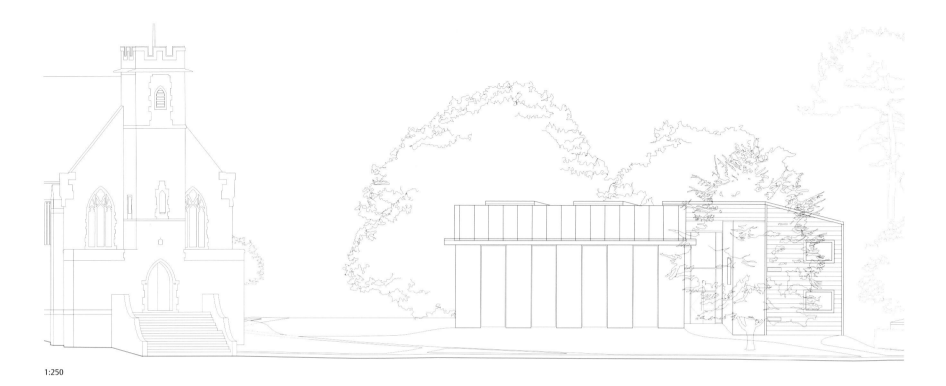

1:250

above: West elevation seen from the sports field. The listed school chapel by GF Bodley is to the left and the low-lying rifle range to the right.

The school's Chapel follows a standard liturgical pattern with its east–west orientation, its west front with its broad set of steps is perhaps a subconscious amalgam of Oxbridge chapel typology and ancient Greek temple emplacement. Very distant echoes might be heard in the Chapel's subdued late utilitarian Victorian-Gothic reiteration (by GF Bodley, 1907) of such eidetic instances as the linear King's College Chapel, 1446–1515. Given this context, the site for the new complex for Bedford School's Music School has been a challenge. Not quite reaching the building line of the playing fields, that is, not being allowed to play in the front line with the Great Hall as the architecturally unfortunate science complex and the Chapel, the Music School nevertheless knows how to maximise its formal presence.

Eric Parry Architects appear to have been challenged by the site's limitations, turning these to the building's advantage. Rather than being pressed hard against the system of paths at the edge of the playing field, the setback building line provides breathing space, an opportunity to create an aura through archaic landscape elements as the triple grass terrace. This is used in combination with the large overhang for external performances of the school's orchestra (the functional explanation), but more significantly from the point of view of the architectural intention, as an abstraction of ancient Greek *crepidoma* (the stepped platform of Greek temples). The Music School's principal space, the recital hall for an audience of about 140 people, is treated in this spirit: a contemporary reinterpretation of an ancient Greek temple.

Bedford School's relocation in 1891 from the town centre to the extensive backwaters of a very large suburban site secured them the room for necessary development areas in the outgoing nineteenth century. However, the school's fathers were unlikely to have foreseen the development and shift in planning law in favour of the *status quo*. Parts of Bedford School are reachable only through the side lanes and back alleys of late Victorian villas; the Music School is approached from Kimbolton Road down one of these alleys. Reaching agreement with these neighbours on new developments is in itself a major achievement, let alone the construction of a new piece of architecture. One of the consequences from these negotiations determined the number and size of windows on the eastern part of the building complex so as to protect the neighbours' privacy.

In an analogous move, the distribution of the Music School's programme followed this notion of securing the privacy and individuality of the musician on the eastern side to the enabling of the communal experience of both performers and audience on the western side. The contextual composition follows an urban metaphor: the three parts of the Music School's programme are gathered around a double-height, almost external "street space" (EPA's term). The teaching block,

ground floor

1. recital hall
2. lecture room
3. percussion room
4. practice room
5. staff room
6. small teaching room
7. assist. dom.
8. strings storage
9. ensemble room
10. secretary
11. director of music
12. pupil's Instrumental Stow
13. music school garden
14. street
15. entrances

first floor

1. recital hall below
2. ict room
3. recording / control room
4. rock room
5. practice room
6. head of wind teaching room
7. small teaching room
8. head of brass teaching room
9. small music store
10. head of strings teaching room
11. head of piano teaching room
12. street space below
13. library
14. existing mature yew

1:250

below: Cutaway perspective showing the relationship of the double-height spaces, the recital hall and street, to the cellular nature of the practice rooms (accessible at all time thus incorporating the lift) and teaching rooms.

The solid stainless steel piers of the recital hall incorporate a structural frame (1), ventilation (lower section) (2), and variable acoustic panels (upper section) (3). The west and south elevations incorporate external stainless steel roller blinds for solar control (4). Radiant heating panels (dotted) are set at variable angles for acoustic modelling (5).

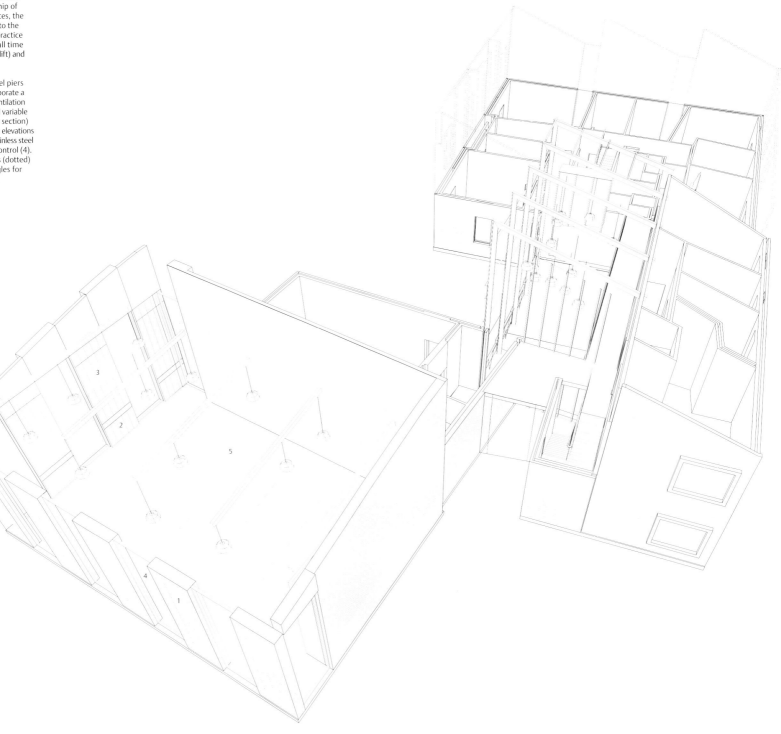

left: View looking east. The street space economically roofed and clad using a Dutch greenhouse system giving the school an informal practice space. The building uses, like the library, the existing site contours to minimise excavation and the street is ramped.

right: View of the street looking west. The gallery connects the practice rooms to the west with the teaching rooms to the east. At ground level the wall under is used as an instrument store and incorporates a handrail at mid-level.

opposite left: Interior of the recital hall looking out towards the school chapel.

opposite right: Exterior of recital hall. The cantilevered overhang provides shading and a contrasting weight to the vertical panels. The grass berm overlooking the sports field can also be used for informal events.

replacing an Edwardian villa that EPA determined was unable to meet the standards of acoustic insulation (both internal as well as external), the practice wing and the recital hall thus form three relatively distinct configurations. Although separated by flash gaps, entrance recesses or double-storey glazing, the three configurations are unified by the variegated stretcher bond brickwork, that here more clearly continues the patina and picturesque brickwork of the school's central buildings than the library.

Although the recital hall is all but separated from the "street space", that is to say, it is almost its own configuration; its object quality is tempered by the continuation of brickwork to the south facade as well as to the adjacent lecture room. Thus the temple front extends on the west and north facades only, the dominant front being the western one. Here five vertical panels of 4 mm bead-blasted, stainless steel cladding panels pre-assembled to a trussed steel frame fulfil a number of tasks. First, they are the principal structural elements on the two sides of the hall. Secondly, they are ducts carrying the air supply to the hall as well as the recesses for adjustable acoustic panels that allow for a wider breadth of sound absorption and reflection. Thirdly, the 5.5 m high and 1.74 m wide panels, set at 1.8 m centres, are readable as abstracted piers, forming a rudimentary, if not archaic, tectonic of thin folded skins. The archaism results also from the odd number of "piers" or tectonic elements; in ancient Greek architecture this was a highly unusual occurrence, for example at the so-called Basilica at Paestum, c. 530 BC, and at the Temple of Zeus at Agrigentum, c. 510–409 BC.

The recital hall thus does not privilege a central axis (along either direction); its principal entrance underlines its rotational flow. The arrangement of stainless piers too follows this rotational movement. Thus, while from the outside the west facade suggest a static character to the hall, in fact, when standing inside the hall, two directions are competing with each other: the more obvious view to the west, supported also by the sloping ceiling (principally for acoustic reasons to avoid parallel surfaces), against the view to the north as weighted by the corner entrance and thus the conventional arrangement for the seating layout.

The skin-like treatment of the piers is further underlined when external stainless steel louvres are lowered to provide shading for the recital hall. Here, the resulting image on the exterior plays with the observers' perception and basic knowledge of building. In the process of abstraction, multiple readings become possible if the resulting composition alludes to a number of archetypes, be they in the field of configurations or tectonics.

The abstracted facade could also be argued to continue Ètienne-Louis Boullée's idea of an architecture, where shadow creates the basis of cognition. In the design for a funerary monument, Boullée speaks of an architecture of shadows ("*Monument funéraire, caractérisant Le Genre De L'architectrure des Ombres*", c. 1782). In this abstracted temple, in which the orders are reduced to mere piers and voids take the place of the tectonic members, thereby logically requiring a solid pier to take the location on the central axis, Boullée instantiates his idea of the most lugubrious monument consisting of a plane, naked and barren surface, of a light-absorbing material that is absolutely stripped of any detail and whose ornamentation is created by a range of shadows themselves created from even more sombre shadows.[1] EPA's stainless steel cladding panels, readable as massive piers does not fully match this description, most importantly; the stainless steel is not light absorbing. However, in its light reflecting nature, EPA have taken the notion of the architecture of shadows to an architecture of reflection, a quality that is further developed in the office building Aldermanbury Square in the City of London, 2004–2007.

The large "shot-peened" stainless steel panels have a subtle reflective quality, neither shiny nor glaring but mildly light reflective. From a distance a folded sheet may thus look more solid than an untreated or even polished sheet. The cladding panels at the recital hall have a massive appearance, no detail gives away the fact that here we are looking at a 4 mm folded sheet, only a test by knocking on the surface reveals the real nature of the material. Thus the multiple readings that these elements permit move the basic architectural statement away from the literal corporeality of loadbearing stonework seen at 30 Finsbury Square to an "ambiguous" corporeality of the order of an elaborate, multivalent metaphor, or metaphysical conceit.[2]

The resultant composition of the Music School is almost a painterly collage of metaphors: the two-storey, brickwork clad teaching block recalls the Edwardian villa, yet the saw-tooth roof removes it from the domestic world to an institutional one; the "street space" is an urban in intention, while the three configurations are conceived as parts of a Georgian house; the grand recital hall is enclosed on two sides with elements of an ambiguous corporeality while the other two sides are clad in brick, respectively contain services or a meeting room. The notion of collage, as for example the Erechtheion, c. 420–406 BC,

above left: Recital Hall, exterior view in use on a winter afternoon.

above right: Recital hall. The opening of the music school by Peter Maxwell Davies, seated centre front row, who made a passionate case for the importance of music in the development of creativity and self-respect in education.

opposite: The street and the Recital Hall teaching rooms seen from the court garden and retained yew tree.

1:250

on the Athenian Acropolis exemplifies the complex resolution of different programmatic parts, each also addressing the context in specific ways. EPA's Music School faces three sides (the southern one being adjacent to neighbouring gardens or service sheds), while also nestling amongst mature trees that the designers wanted to retain as far as possible. The latter concern in part explains the non-orthogonal plan figure of the complex; more significantly, the west facade of the Recital Hall mediates between the orientations of the Great Hall and the Chapel. The architecture of the Music School synthesises the local needs and programmatic requirements in a highly differentiated collage, so that the resultant volume challenges neither the existing school buildings nor the neighbouring villas, while nevertheless making a distinct appearance as close to the playing field as possible. The building complex thus clearly expresses EPA's carefully balanced approach to highly sensitive sites.

above: Section A–A west–east, showing the combination of cellular and double-height spaces, and the 'settling' of the building into the contours of the site.

opposite: View of the Recital Hall at night.

[1] Boullée, Étienne-Louis, *Tractat d'Architecture, Essai sur l'Art*, Paris 1795 "une surface plane, nue et dépouillée, d'une matière absorbant la lumière, absolument dénuée de détails et dont la décoration est formée par un tableau d'ombres dessiné par des ombres encore plus sombres".

[2] Ambiguous in this context is meant in the differentiated sense of William Empson's *Seven Types of Ambiguity*, London, 1930, 1991, pp. 7–21.

Wimbledon School of Art

Spaces for creative endeavour in the visual arts, music and performance provide the most fertile ground for design research in the broader fields of architecture and urban design. Wimbledon School of Art has been an important project because of both its educational ambition and the artist staff members directing it. Bill Furlong, John Mitchell, Rod Bugg amongst many and a memory that Prunella Clough, niece and confidante of Eileen Gray, taught for many years at the school.

1:2500

above: Site plan showing confines of the site and the connections between the 1930s building (1) and the new facilities (2).

Sketch proposals.

above right: First proposal: Section through studios with wall to the lecture space beyond. This was before neighbours forced a planning appeal that the School lost.

below right: Second proposal: Studios are moved further away from the nearby houses which creates the vertical emphasis that became the wall for John Mitchell's *Asymmetric and Inverted Frustrums*.

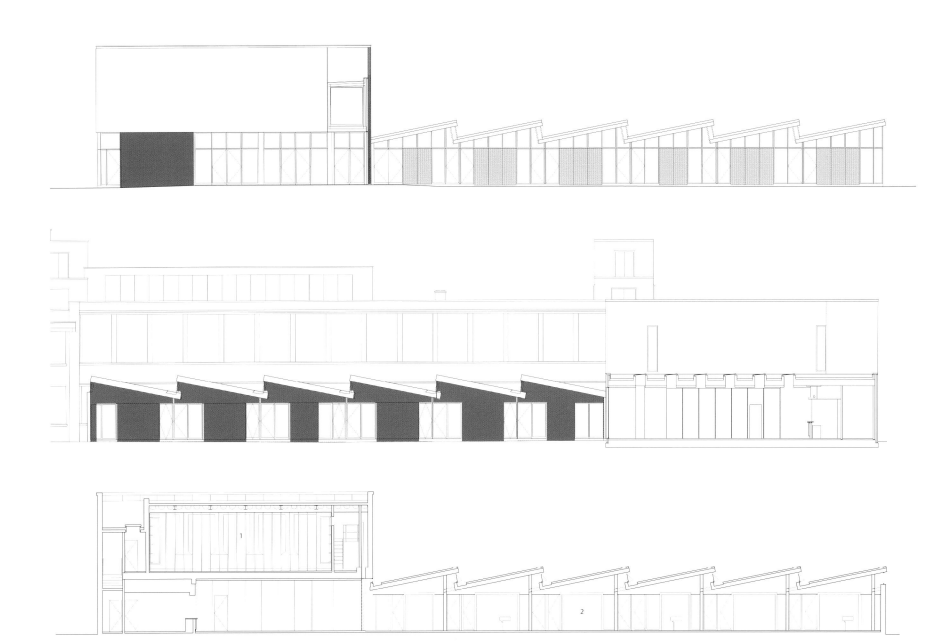

top: East elevation.

middle: West elevation.

bottom: South section.

1. lecture / installation space
2. studios

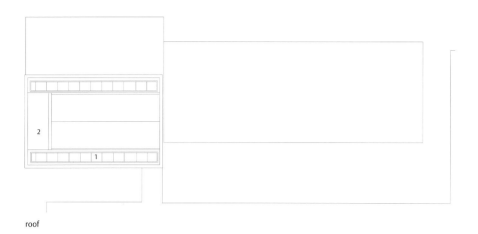

roof

1. skylights
2. attenuater air-handling plant for assisted ventilation

opposite: View of the new studio wing with north lights and a goal-post structure at 6 m centres creating a clear span of 11 m and a room which is 36 m long.

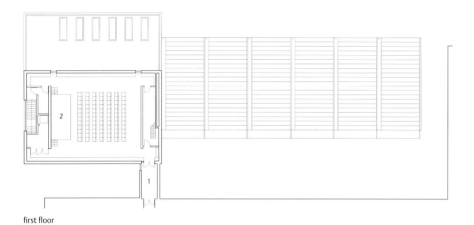

first floor

1. bridge link to existing building
2. lecture / installation space

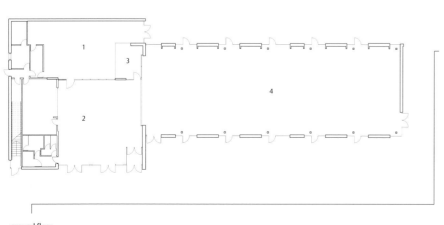

ground floor

1. common room
2. canteen
3. office
4. studios

1:500

Left: View of the first floor lecture/installation space. Not unlike a television studio the space is acoustically isolated with skylights that can be blacked out. Ventilation is mechanically assisted.

opposite left: Typical eaves detail to the south elevation of the ground floor studios.

opposite right: Section of the goalpost structure, north light and uplighters.

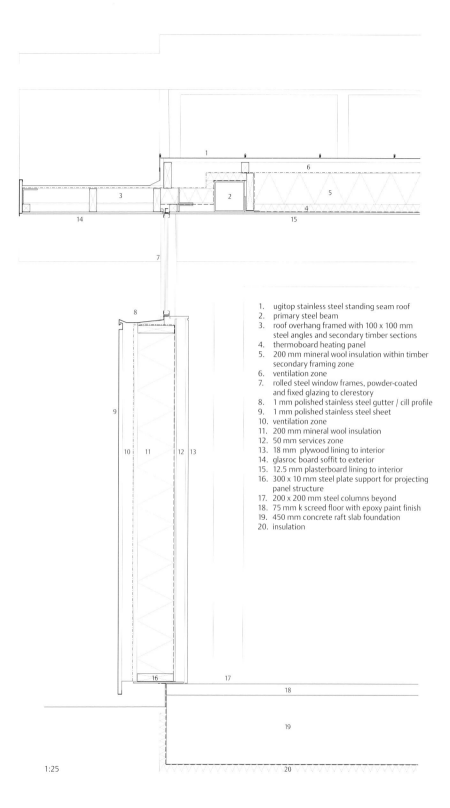

1. ugitop stainless steel standing seam roof
2. primary steel beam
3. roof overhang framed with 100 x 100 mm steel angles and secondary timber sections
4. thermoboard heating panel
5. 200 mm mineral wool insulation within timber secondary framing zone
6. ventilation zone
7. rolled steel window frames, powder-coated and fixed glazing to clerestory
8. 1 mm polished stainless steel gutter / cill profile
9. 1 mm polished stainless steel sheet
10. ventilation zone
11. 200 mm mineral wool insulation
12. 50 mm services zone
13. 18 mm plywood lining to interior
14. glasroc board soffit to exterior
15. 12.5 mm plasterboard lining to interior
16. 300 x 10 mm steel plate support for projecting panel structure
17. 200 x 200 mm steel columns beyond
18. 75 mm k screed floor with epoxy paint finish
19. 450 mm concrete raft slab foundation
20. insulation

1:25

1. primary steel beam
2. 200 x 200 mm rhomboid steel beam
3. 10 x 200 mm steel flats at 3 m centres
4. 200 mm insulation within timber secondary framing zone.
5. ugitop stainless steel lined gutter
6. 50 mm thermoboard heating panels
7. ugitop stainless steel stanging seam roof
8. ugitop stainless steel fascia
9. polyester powder-coated double glazed roof light
10. ventilation zone
11. 12.5 mm skimmed plasterboard

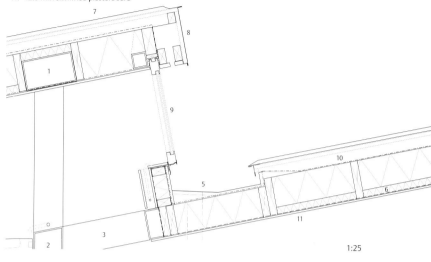

1:25

The brief was to create a studio space, canteen, student hub and lecture room. The main constraint was the limited site area, set between the 1930s art school and the surrounding suburban development. A two-storey structure was permissible only on the southwest part of the site, which adjoins a cul de sac and garages, rather than facing dwellings. Despite the benefits to the school, the scheme was opposed by local residents, which led to a modification in the position of the studios.

The lecture space needed to be readily usable for installation work involving sound and film and therefore needed to be acoustically isolated. This was a brief developed by Bill Furlong whose teaching, extraordinary archive, Audio Arts, and sound sculptures gave a clear spacial direction. The elevated first floor position suited this separation while the bridge link acts as a light and sound lobby between the existing building with its accessible lift and new facilities. Structurally separation was achieved by an in-situ concrete slab to provide a flat solid floor, free from vibration. The 14 m span achieved by this slab also allowed for a large flexible canteen and bar space below. At ground floor the two-storey block is connected to the studios by means of a rising wall.

The studios are roofed by a series of tilted planes that allow north light into the space. They are supported by a truss and 'goalposts' spanning 12 m. The centres between these are at 6 m and reflect the scale of space required for a student, traditionally defined by 8 x 4 foot sheets

top: View of the new studio wing, from the upper floor of the existing art school building.

bottom: Opposite view looking towards the existing building.

opposite: Typical student bay within the ground floor studios.

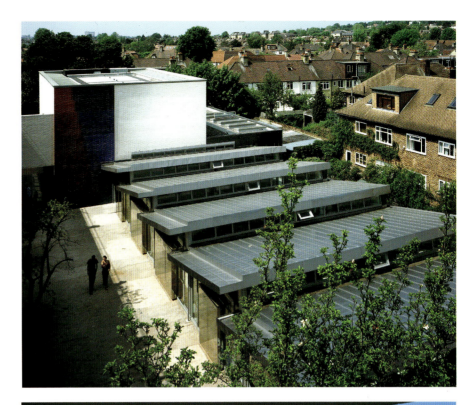

of ply or mdf. For events such as the end-of-year exhibition, a clear 12 x 40 m space can be created which, if the wall is raised, increases in length to 60 m.

The courtyard elevation to the studios is made from metal-framed doors and windows. These are set between polished stainless steel blocks which contain wet services and alleviate the proximity to the existing building by their reflectivity and lightness. All the artificial lighting and heating are contained in the soffit, which contains a low temperature water system in it, rather than in the floor, where it would be prone to damage from fixings, etc.. A low-energy strategy was developed, focusing on passive measures where possible, by making best use of daylight, thermal mass and natural ventilation and, where more active systems were needed, by ensuring energy efficient design. The artificial lighting scheme was designed to complement the architectural intent.

Timothy Taylor Gallery

Founded in 1996, the gallery started life in a former storage space in Bruton Place remodelled by Thomas Croft, moving to Dering Street in 2003 occupying space designed by Eric Parry Architects. The most recent move to Carlos Place in 2007 is a direct consequence of the irrepressible commercial forces in the London property market, obliging even successful gallerists to relocate at short notice.

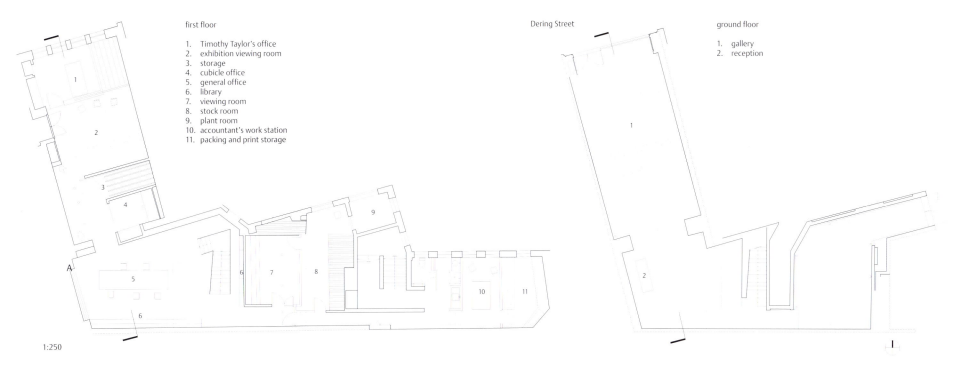

first floor

1. Timothy Taylor's office
2. exhibition viewing room
3. storage
4. cubicle office
5. general office
6. library
7. viewing room
8. stock room
9. plant room
10. accountant's work station
11. packing and print storage

Dering Street

ground floor

1. gallery
2. reception

1:250

opposite: View of the ground floor gallery towards rear wall. Precast steps to the first floor are visible, centre. Sean Scully exhibition, 2003.

above: Gallery floor plans.

right: View of ground floor gallery from the Dering Street entrance.

In fact, both the Bruton Place and the Dering Street premises had been galleries before, the latter occupied by Anthony D'Offay since 1980, whose sudden closure in 2002 prompted a major commercial and spatial realignment in the London gallery scene.

For both the gallerist as well as the architect, the move into an existing gallery raises expectations. Gallery program, list of artists, quality of lighting, movement, manner of display and presentation to private collectors are some aspects on which gallerist and architect place distinct accents. Taking on the premises of one of the most renowned art gallerists of the last two decades of the twentieth-century, the Timothy Taylor Gallery itself created a venue for largely young non-British art in its new premises in Dering Street. It occupied a complex site with a two-storey L-shaped configuration. In its mix of static and irregular geometries, the spaces formed a so-called project space, which embraced traditional hanging of art as well as installation work.

The main change to the D'Offay gallery was the insertion of a prefabricated concrete stair, not dissimilar to Álvaro Siza's Porto Art Gallery, 1973–1974 (now destroyed), in which the staircase was expressive of the connection between ground floor and basement. The stair in the Timothy Taylor Gallery was subtly tapered to form an almost unnoticeable trompe l'œil. The general attitude in the design reflects this notion of contemporary discretion. Members of the interested

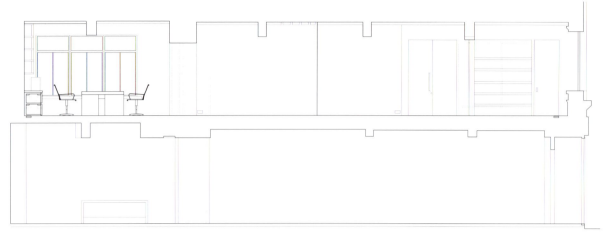

1:250

top left: Section A–A

top right: The art fair desk designed for Timothy Taylor has to reconcile several requirements: stability, portability, simplicity and erectability. Dismountable solid surface panels stiffen a stainless steel spine and pack into a case to travel between international Art Fairs.

bottom left: Passage leading to Timothy Taylor's office, with cubicle room and storage racks beyond.

bottom right: General office viewed from the top of the stairs.

opposite: View of the library in the general office with stairs rising from the ground floor gallery.

left and opposite:
Tony Smith exhibition, 2004.

public were able to wander around the three spaces without feeling too aware of the gallery representative at the reception in the bend of the space. The entrance room was the most regular, the other two quasi-larger circulation areas.

At the newly concentrated office spaces on the first floor the service areas from storage to packaging were kept behind a door in the long wing, while gallery attendants were able to show potential buyers selected work in three separately accessible spaces, the largest being immediately connected to Timothy Taylor's own office facing Dering Street. The architectural character of the upper level then continued the attitude of the casually discrete: the entire series of spaces centred on the general office could be sensed as a loose concatenation.

With regard to the choice of materials and furnishings, the mute palate of colours and surface textures favoured by international modernist galleries found its way into the Timothy Taylor Gallery too. The newly cast and polished screed floor at ground level was deliberately allowed to show tone-in-tone irregularities so as not to overwhelm by means of its extensively homogeneous presence. In this, the Timothy Taylor Gallery shares the aesthetic preference established in Donald Judd's adaptations of typical Texan building stock in Marfa from the early 1970s. The post-military and post-industrial environments, so often favoured by artists, were given a purified lease of life as exhibition spaces for large, difficult to install pieces of art.

The exposed beams, irregular wall enclosures, changes in floor levels of the Timothy Taylor Gallery are a far cry from the archetypal notion of the perfectly orthogonally composed series of spaces. In this, the Taylor Gallery is closer to Gluckman Mayner's Andrea Rosen and Luhring Augustine Galleries in New York City of 1998. There, the existing structural elements are not seen as an annoying problem that interfere with the contemplation of art, but on the contrary, the architectural equivalent of sound's white noise.

The Timothy Taylor Gallery thus offered a balance between the discrete charm of the carefully careless and the siren calls of minimalist abstraction. Perhaps this is most clearly borne out by the quality of artificial lighting. The walls were allowed to be accentuated by sectional washers rather than to provide a shadowless consistency sought by more purist art galleries. Perhaps too, it could be said that the very choice of the premises, with its unusual urban geometry, already predisposed the design in this direction. However, as other architects have shown in the past, both modern and traditional, the interpretation of the given space can transcend the pre-existing restrictions.

Particularly on the upper level, Eric Parry Architects' new design signalled a merger between neo-Plasticist spatial potential (sliding panels for art in the more ambiguous circulation area) and the tradition of cellular space (for example, Sir John Soane's studio in Lincoln Inn's Fields) on the totally enclosed viewing room.

185 Park Street

The transformation of Bankside over the last 15 years makes a fascinating study in urban renewal. Some of the first seeds were sown with the debate and set of small projects exhibited at the Future Southwark exhibition 1996 (Volume 1). The creative decision by the Tate to occupy Gilbert Scott's disused power station coupled with the realisation of the Millennium Bridge and the earlier development of the Globe Theatre have created a massive public presence in what was a wasteland, albeit with pockets of housing and warehousing.

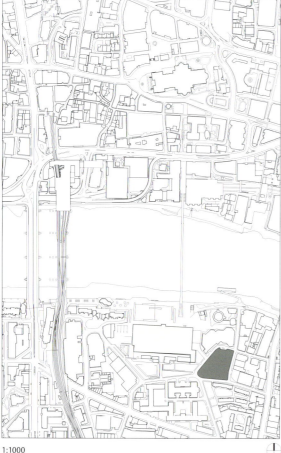

1:1000

left: Site model illustrating the plan form of the three buildings.

bottom left: Site plan.

opposite:
1. Office building with retail space at ground level. Conceived as a multi-tenanted office the building was developed with two lightwells and separate lift cores, accessible from independent entrance lobbies. A flat slab concrete structure cantilevers to the perimeter upstand beam creating the strong continuous ribbon glazing and horizontal emphasis.

2. Residential tower with double-height retail space at ground level. The apartments accessed off an open lift and stair core are set out parallel to the base of the triangle with balconies in the residual spaces from the sides of the plan. The walls of the building are loadbearing interlocking precast concrete panels on an in-situ concrete 'table'.

3. Brick residential building. This smaller building responds to the existing housing estate to the south in scale and the proportions of openings. It also masks the larger office building to the north, reinforcing the domestic character of Sumner Street.

There has been an escalating sequence of projects with the ripple effect of urban regeneration in London, the largest of which will be the post-Olympic transformation of Stratford and the Lea Valley. It was the provocative tactics of the Architecture Foundation, led at that time by Ricky Burdett, which gave rise to the London Debates during one of which Tony Blair as part of New Labour's drive for election pledged to create a Mayor for London alongside broader plans for devolution. Southwark's dual scalp of housing the Greater London Authority and Tate Modern on its soil has created a case study in urban renewal.

The lure of a new cultural quarter wetted developers appetites and the consequences of the feast are mixed in quality. 185 Park Street, as the street name implies, lies at the corner of an ancient deer park west of the bear pits and theatres of Southwark. It is now an important one and a quarter acre site, just south and east of Tate. The existing buildings were built as the headquarters of the National Grid in the 1960s and pay no heed to the geometry of the site leaving almost the entire boundary of the site inaccessible, fenced and with a perimeter given over to car parking.

The owners Chelsfield, decided to run an architectural competition. The question for the competition was how to turn this isolation into a mixed-use responsive neighbour to the south of Tate Modern. The emergence of what was to be called the three-in-one scheme: a tall triangular residential building at the eastern apex of the site, a large office building re-establishing the site boundary to Park Street and Emerson Street and a mirroring of the scale of the Estate housing to the south to create the beginnings of a dialogue in Sumner Street.

right: Sketch illustrating the emerging idea of the contrast between vertical and horizontal characterisation.

left: Typical floor.

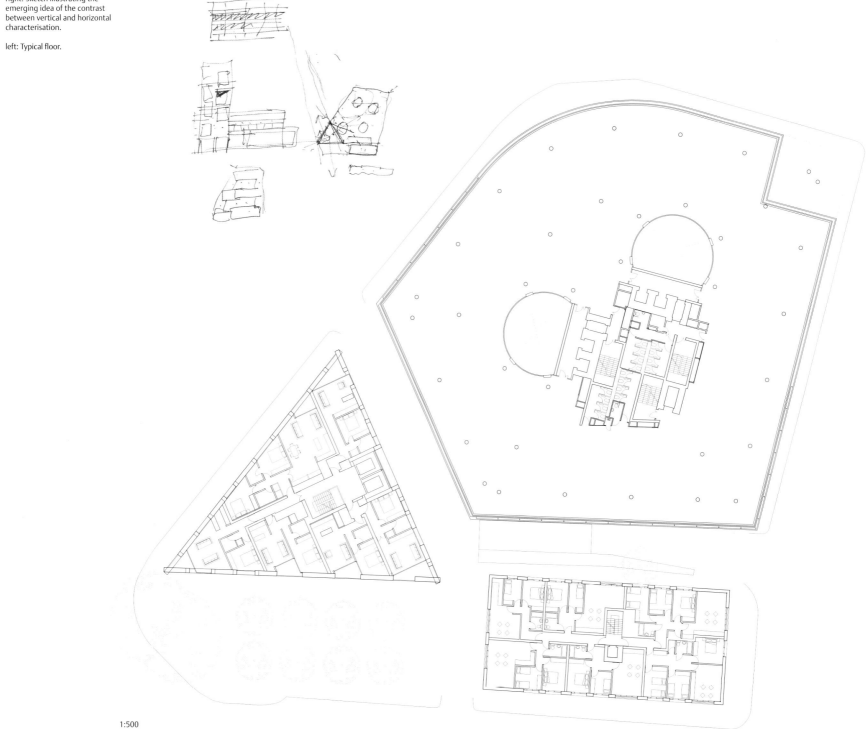

1:500

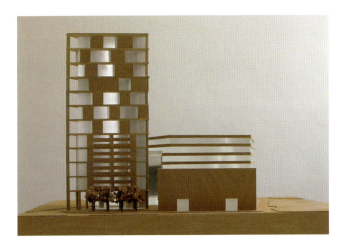

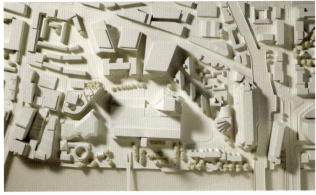

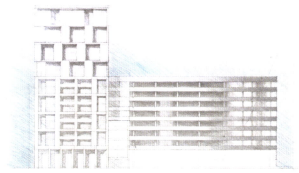

Elevations studies and model. Site model showing the cyclorama-like sweep of buildings to the south of Tate Modern, creating an important new public space and threshold from the south.

The 24-storey residential building is articulated and broken down with a two-storey height order, the structural walls a composition of precast concrete panels stack like a 'house of cards'. These dark panels give the building a visual weight set next to the dour horizontality of the old power station. The balconies and glazed elements were to be made up of a palette of glass and polished metal finishes which would sparkle like gems within the dark carapace.

The office block is, in contrast to the verticality of the residential building, a series of horizontal ribbons. The facade is conceived as a series of trays formed with a structural concrete upstand with uninterrupted ribbon windows. At the seventh floor there is a set-back providing a terrace, which will be an amenity for all users of the building.

The facades of the residential building are proposed to be made of brick, as are the residential blocks to the south, in particular Sumner Buildings directly opposite. The roof is also to be finished with an undulating brick surface, so seen from the upper storeys of the residential block, the building reads as a material whole. At ground floor level the building will incorporate community uses, such as a crèche, which opens onto the new public space to the west.

At an urban scale, the block is split into a number of elements creating two new pedestrian routes and activating the perimeter with a series of new entrances and uses. The grouping creates a focal point at the southwest corner of the site with the residential tower.

top: South elevation of the proposal in the context of Tate Modern.

Bottom: Northwest elevation along Park Street.

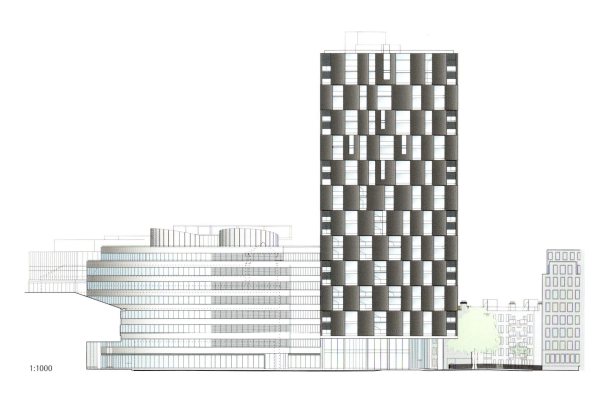

1:1000

right: Model view of the residential tower from Tate Modern extension. A dark carapace with the jewel-like sparkle of stainless steel framing the fenestration and balconies within.

below: Death by deliberations. Sketches of the planning appeal which the developer lost but with commendation of much of the proposals.

5 Aldermanbury Square

Eric Parry Architects has a reputation for resolving some of the most contested urban and architectural issues. The practice unfailingly demonstrates both their profound understanding of the specific contextual history and their grounding in the discourse of architecture that extends beyond the text-book reduction of modernist heroes.

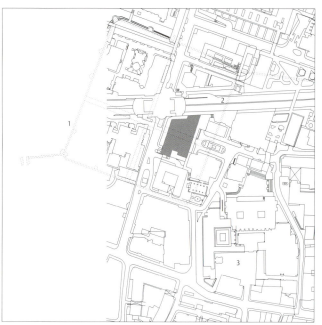

far left: East elevation of Royex House prior to demolition. The horizontal emphasis is created by the ribbons of glazing and spandrel panels which was the hallmark of 60s curtain walling systems.

left: Site plan of the building with the dotted outline of the Roman fort of Londinium (1). London Wall (2) cuts obliquely across the Roman and Medieval street pattern. The Guildhall Yard (3) lies to the southeast and frames an important view of the building, which was one of the generators for the vertical emphasis of the building.

opposite left: View from the high walk on the north side of Wood Street, with a Medieval bastion on the line of the Roman fort wall in the foreground. The Corporation Police Headquarters tower lies on a perpendicular axis to the south. The exaggerated verticality of the corner is a result of the acute angle of London Wall to the building's juxtaposition against the entasis that develops over the top eight storeys.

opposite right: View southwards down Wood Street from Alban Gate high walk. The pavement and passage under the building was occupied by a ramped access to the Barbican high walk level. This has been incorporated to current standards on the north flank of the building.

No surprise then that the practice should be commissioned by the clients of 30 Finsbury Square, Scottish Widows (this time together with Teacher's Insurance) to design an 18-storey high-rise office on London Wall.

To the north of the site stands Terry Farrell's ungainly "Alban Gate" on London Wall, 1987–1992); to the west is 88 Wood Street, a decent speculative office development by Richard Rogers partnership, 1994–1998); and next to this is Norman Foster's unspectacular speculative office low-rise at 100 Wood Street, 2000. To the south of the site stands the remarkable Police Headquarters by McMorran & Whitby, 1966, and right in the middle of Wood Street the remnant tower of St Alban's Church by Christopher Wren, 1685, is located. Finally, to the east is the Hall of the Worshipful Company of Brewers. A few yards beyond these distinct neighbours, there is the Guild Hall itself, from whose court No 5 is distinctly visible, thankfully screening "Alban Gate".

Were these buildings the only ones to which one might refer as a contemporary architect, then they themselves would suffice as a thesaurus of high-rise architecture. In its contextualist configuration, 88 Wood Street sets a reasonable benchmark for the ongoing transformation of the fabric of the city. The irony of this is that the building to which it was deferring with its lower section, was replaced by a subsequent building of equal height as its predecessor. Terry Farrell's "Alban Gate" represents the insatiable force of developers and the pragmatic lenience of the Corporation's planning laws. Postmodernism or not, probably no architectural order or language is able to bring a conceptual discipline to bear on the permissible envelope for this site. The result is monstrous. "Alban Gate" is by no means a unique occurrence in the City; it is symptomatic of the hybrid situation in which much development in the City of London finds itself: on the one hand, the attempt to adhere to the existing street profile that renders the configuration the result of public space versus the tendency of tall buildings to seek autonomy, both for functional reasons such as daylighting as well as for representational reasons. The rules for rights of light, however, are remarkably flexible in the City of London. Medieval regulations favour dense adjacencies, and it is not uncommon that a tenant of a high-rise, who has enjoyed panoramic views from the rented offices, is confronted a few years later by an equally tall building, now blocking the view.

The modernist configuration of podium and tower generally does not work in the City of London, at least not with a recognisable podium of something of a regular geometric profile. McMorran & Whitby's Police Headquarters is an exception in this regard. Not at all conforming to the notion of podium and slab, the design treats low- and high-rise elements of the same building in a coherent manner without recourse to the modernist sleight of hand: from an orthogonal courtyard one

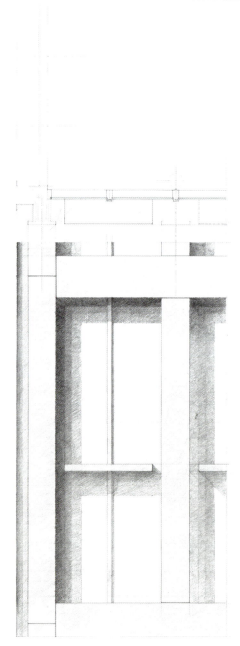

left: Aluminium model at scale 1:50. Ultimately with tighter engineering of the structure an extra floor was achieved almost within the original height agreement and gave rise to the triple bay of the lower floor levels above the raised public area.

below: Preliminary facade study.

Sequence of development models from left: Original model of Royex House—note ramp on Wood Street. Staggered wings and massing two rectilinear wings and central section. Ideal proportions, discussions with Peter Reese moderated the height but confirmed the symmetrical height of the two wings rather than a building that stepped to the street cornice like the west side Wood Street buildings do.

of the sides rises to form a narrow slab of 14 storeys. The self-assured continuation of a condensed classicism here, influenced by Edwin Lutyens, creates a credible solution to the compositional strains of reconciling lower and taller elements. The towering element itself exhibits the subtle refinement of Greek entasis. The facade of every second floor is set back with respect to the lower pair by a minute dimension. On the whole, the police station benefits from its freestanding condition, thus not having to adapt the clarity of the square court to the haphazard plots of Medieval London.

As an alternative strategy for the insertion of high-rises in the dense City, the Miesian approach of a public space and tower, on the other hand, has worked; see for example the former Commercial Union Tower (now Aviva Tower, at 1 Undershaft) by Collins Melvin Ward & Partners, 1968–1969, although it has meant the clearance of the smaller grained historic fabric. Of course, the success of this strategy depends upon the continued existence of at least some of the small grained historic development, otherwise, the continued development along the lines of say New York's Sixth Avenue will result in the same banality.

The envelope permissible for Eric Parry Architects' design on Aldermanbury Square fortunately for the investor allowed for a more or less straightforward 18-storey high-rise. The new high-rise replaces Royex House, 1962, a narrow slab of 16 m width by Richard Seifert. Located on the west side of Aldermanbury Square, the long eastern facade forms a dominant enclosure to the newly remodelled square, beneficiary of the Corporation's attempt at improving public spaces in the Square Mile, its so-called "Street Scene Challenge" programme. The design of the remodelled square is by EPA and was funded by the developers of 5 Aldermanbury

and other proximate developments through Section 106 of the Town and Country Planning Act (1990), otherwise known as "planning gain". Part of this remodelling of the square is the creation of a public pedestrian route at ground floor level across the site of the high-rise. On the west facade, the high-rise forms a tall enclosure to Wood Street. To the north, with the convolutions of London Wall, with its post-World War II nonsense of separated pedestrian and vehicular traffic (that spills over from the Barbican Estate), the new building offers little relief to "Alban Gate".

Though the effective width of EPA's high-rise is some 36 m, by means of a subdivision of the mass akin to Hentrich, Petschnigg & Partner's Thyssen high-rise in Düsseldorf (23 m wide, 1957–1960), which is a purer version of the abstracted planar shift than Harrison & Abramowitz' earlier Alcoa Building in Pittsburgh (30 m wide, 1951–1953), the south facing configuration is divided into three sections, the central one being recessed and formed into a sweeping vertical gesture that allows an increased penetration of daylight into the depths of the building. Most noticeably, however, is the gentle curve that has been placed on both long elevations of the high-rise. Here, EPA are determining a definitive conclusion to an otherwise endlessly expandable constructional concept—the high-rise. With the superimposition of the tapering effect of entasis, as for the classical orders, the convex tapering of the configuration reaches its cultural conclusion, not its constructional termination. As has been mentioned, the neighbouring Police Headquarters of McMorran & Whitby displays the same gesture, albeit more subtle and one that Eric Parry has acknowledged himself as having been inspired by Edwin Lutyens Cenotaph in Whitehall, 1919–1920, the joint source for both EPA as for McMorran & Whitby.[1] Significantly for both the high-rise component of the Police Headquarters as for

147

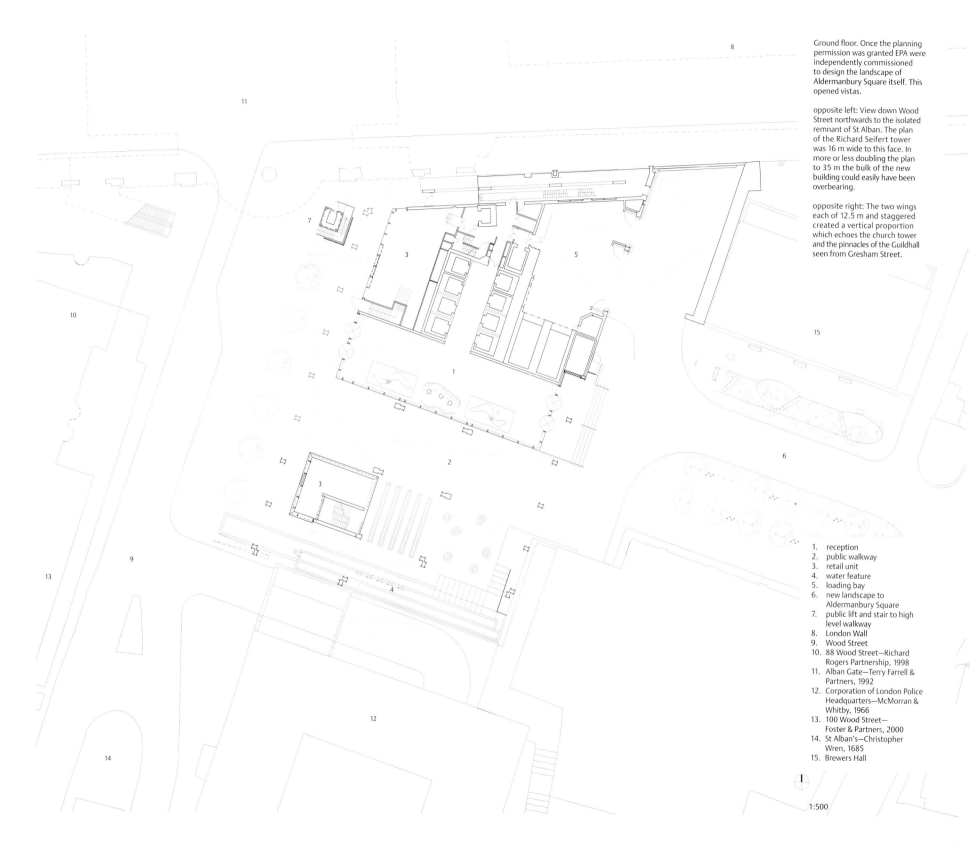

Ground floor. Once the planning permission was granted EPA were independently commissioned to design the landscape of Aldermanbury Square itself. This opened vistas.

opposite left: View down Wood Street northwards to the isolated remnant of St Alban. The plan of the Richard Seifert tower was 16 m wide to this face. In more or less doubling the plan to 35 m the bulk of the new building could easily have been overbearing.

opposite right: The two wings each of 12.5 m and staggered created a vertical proportion which echoes the church tower and the pinnacles of the Guildhall seen from Gresham Street.

1. reception
2. public walkway
3. retail unit
4. water feature
5. loading bay
6. new landscape to Aldermanbury Square
7. public lift and stair to high level walkway
8. London Wall
9. Wood Street
10. 88 Wood Street—Richard Rogers Partnership, 1998
11. Alban Gate—Terry Farrell & Partners, 1992
12. Corporation of London Police Headquarters—McMorran & Whitby, 1966
13. 100 Wood Street—Foster & Partners, 2000
14. St Alban's—Christopher Wren, 1685
15. Brewers Hall

1:500

5 Aldermanbury Square, the Cenotaph is a tall, pier-like composition. It is conceived as an abstraction of a classical column, with its base, shaft, capital and architrave transposed into a series of setback parallelepipeds. On the equivalent section of the shaft, there is no curvature; the Cenotaph's entasis effect being essentially realised by the series of setbacks that culminate in the coffin-like abstraction of metopes and triglyphs.

Whereas it is possible to argue that the superimposition of entasis on the high-rise's configuration is merely a formalist game, more significantly, the embodiment of this follows in the tradition of Louis Sullivan's definition of how the "Tall Office Building" should be metaphorically considered.[2] The three-part division, which Sullivan understands both as an organic simile as well as belonging to the greater discourse on architecture reaching as far back as "the Greek temple, the Gothic cathedral, the Medieval fortress". Adolf Loos' literal translation of this notion in his competition entry for the Chicago Tribune Tower has remained a powerful icon for architects interested in the continuation of classical principles of architecture, and Loos' conviction that, "the great Greek Doric column will one day be built. If not in Chicago, then in another city. If not for the 'Chicago Tribune', then for someone else. If not by me, then by some other architect", reflects the certainty of the logical inevitability of the architectural concept.[3] Today, in the age of fragmentation, abstraction and

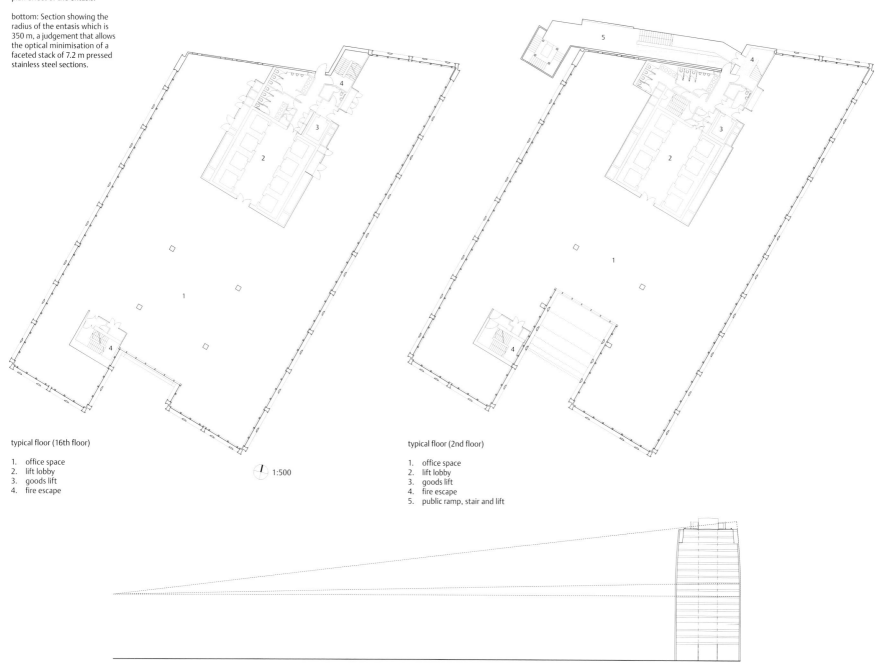

top: Typical floor plans at the lower and upper levels. On the lower levels the belly cuts back between the two wings to allow daylight into the public space below. On the upper levels the plan width decreases with the plan effect of the entasis.

bottom: Section showing the radius of the entasis which is 350 m, a judgement that allows the optical minimisation of a faceted stack of 7.2 m pressed stainless steel sections.

typical floor (16th floor)

1. office space
2. lift lobby
3. goods lift
4. fire escape

typical floor (2nd floor)

1. office space
2. lift lobby
3. goods lift
4. fire escape
5. public ramp, stair and lift

1:500

1:2000

transformation, this conviction could be extended to include: if not as a literal Doric column, then as a variation.

What fluting is to the Doric column, the emphasis on the vertical is to the high-rise tower. Fluting of columns suppresses the constructional fact that the columns consist of individually stacked drums of stone, each of which could be of a different height. In order to overcome this real constraint due to the available size of stone blocks from the quarry as well as a means of unifying the shaft of a column, the highly complex cutting of flutes on a shaft of a column with entasis accentuated its verticality. Thus, for high-rise buildings the entasis is a means of stressing the vertical tectonic elements. There is of course no logical necessity to do so, especially in insulated buildings. On the contrary, the endoskeletal is the more physiologically appropriate in northern climates as it allows for direct avoidance of cold-bridging through which, in very cold weather conditions, the more humid air on the inside can condensate on cold surfaces. In the long term, this can amongst other things cause corrosion on exposed steels of the primary structure. EPA have always enclosed the principal structural elements unless, as in the case of 30 Finsbury Square, the loadbearing material is in itself monolithic and the transition from the exoskeletal frame to the interior is insulated. For 5 Aldermanbury Square, EPA have enveloped the structural Corten hollow rectangular steel sections with shot-peened stainless steel panels. The pattern of this cladding grid accentuates the vertical. With the exception of the first to third floors, every subsequent two floors are paired by a horizontal panel that is set flush with the vertical elements. In addition to this, a freestanding vertical panel subdivides every structural bay. A horizontal sill is fixed at the intermediate floors. A faint echo might be heard from the neighbouring high-rise by McMorran & Whitby: here the architects paired every two floors in the graduated slimming of the volume.

For this high-rise, both the horizontal as well as the vertical tectonic elements were to be clad with milled panels from 1.5 m wide stainless steel coil, which has a direction to its finish. The shot-peening neutralises the surface direction and thereby homogenises the horizontal and vertical cladding components. In their profile, the principle vertical cladding elements to the Corten hollow sections are treated like flanges of I-sections. The intermediate panels take up the "flange" thickness. In concert, the entire cladding system is set some 500 mm from the glazing and in part acts like a large sunscreen.

1. reception
2. public space
3. lookout benches
4. public passage to Love Lane
5. in-situ concrete water wall
    5a rills
    5b rivulet
    5c cast bronze gargoyle
6. entrance to retail / restaurant below pavement
7. Wood Street
8. Aldermanbury Square
9. lift core
10. seats, worktop and rugs
11. textile wall hanging

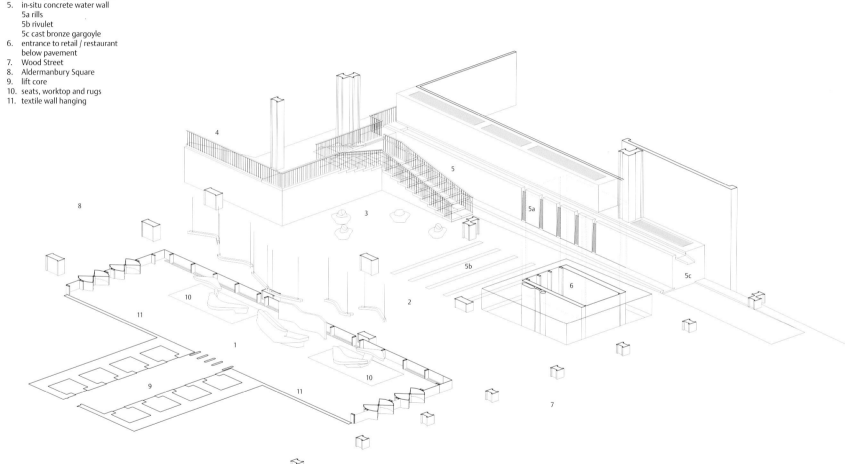

below: Isometric projection of street level.

opposite left: Diagonal view from the level of the high walk from Alban Gate, through the reception glass wall.

opposite right: View to Aldermanbury Square from the public space under the building. In the foreground the water rills and lookout benches.

below: Dusk view from the Barbican looking south to the city with the south elevation of the eastern wing illuminated.

right: West elevation to Aldermanbury Square.

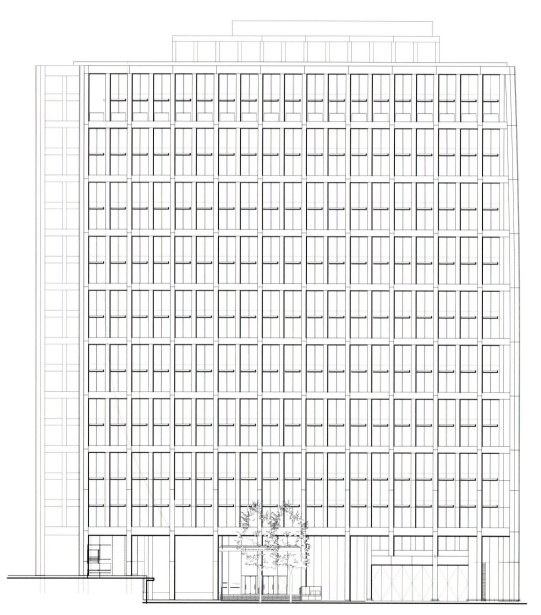

below: East elevation to Wood Street, the inflected north elevation with ramp access to Barbican to the left.

right: South elevation.

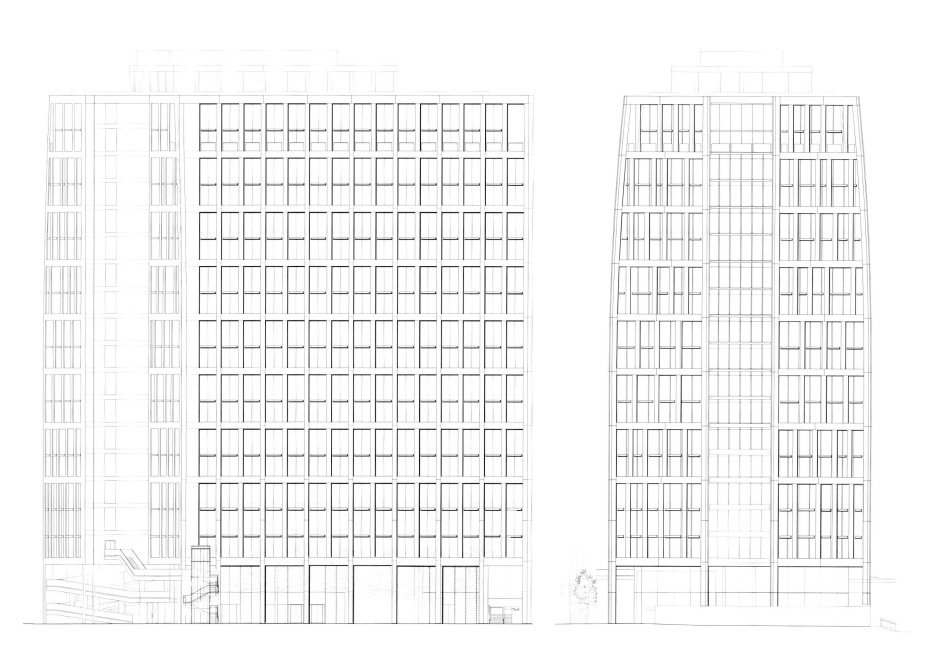

In its effect, it could be regarded as a large-scale warp and weft of steel. The shot-peening is of central importance so as to achieve both a character of neutrality as well as a unified appearance of this "woven" gauze. On the southern facade, the alignment of the vertical panels does not relate to any structural supports and therefore by its picturesque composition, reminiscent only in its seemingly random position of the stone piers of 30 Finsbury Square, speaks of its character as cladding. Furthermore, the picturesque placement of the vertical panels also avoids any awkward chamfered outer bays that might have resulted from the configurational entasis.

Thus, it is precisely because of the creation of flanges to the cladding panels that there is the possibility of reading the entire system as a screen and not as the presence of the actual loadbearing elements. In a sense, the use of such flanges continues Mies van der Rohe's detailing principles, which, as for instance in the Seagram Building, 1954–1958, in turn can be considered a continuation of the sculptural effect of fluting. As is the case with serifs in given typefaces, these accentuate the edges and corners, thereby ensuring clarity and distinction even for small point sizes. The flanges of the vertical bronze I-sections of the Seagram Building create secondary, more delicate recesses than the implied depth created between the front of the flange and the glazing. While Mies van der Rohe's detailing creates a stoic consistency where the dominant surface of the building lies in the plane of the glazing, EPA's

left: View towards Wood Street from the square. The reflective soffit of polished black granite foils the mass of the building above, also visible is the base of the curved belly between the two wings.

above: Preliminary drawing for the lookout bench, an urban perch to accommodate several people without disturbance. Seven of these giant pebbles of contrasting stone are placed under the building.

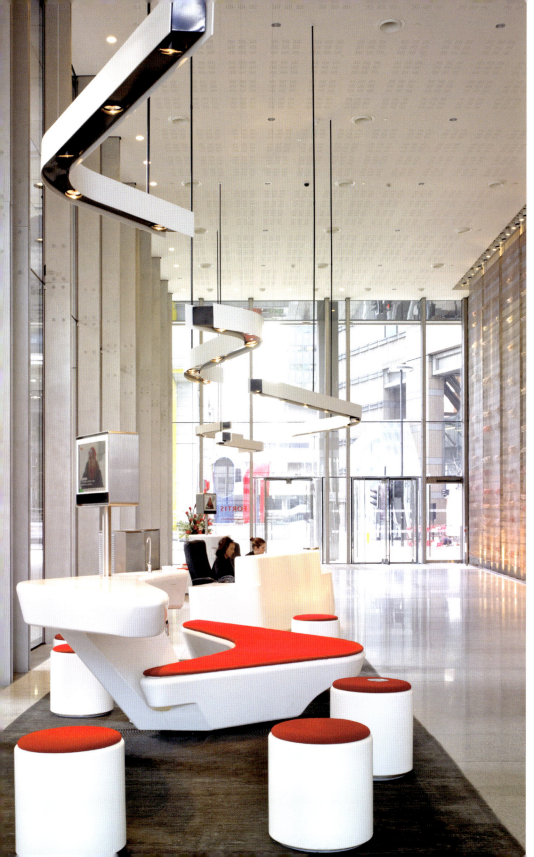

left: View of the reception from the east end. The furniture was designed for informal meeting and waiting.

top right: Initial sketch for the wall textiles with horizons and colour (seen finished to the right in the photograph) hung in front of the in-situ board marked concrete wall leading to the lift lobby.

bottom right: Drawing of the hand knotted rug seen under furniture in the photograph, one of two.

opposite: Skywards view from the new public space under the building with the recess of the 'belly' between the two wings. A corner of the McMorran & Whitby city police headquarters tower is visible.

cladding at 5 Aldermanbury Square asserts as the dominant plane the outer surface of the steel cladding: all the rest is an amalgamated density of shadows and reflections within the depth of half a metre.

That weaving might be considered to be an overriding theme in this development of Aldermanbury Square and could be illuminated by three other, albeit differently scaled experiences. First, the interconnection between Wood Street and Aldermanbury Square via the undercroft of the new high-rise: EPA created a number of conditions that specifically fix the building in its location. Along the southern edge a watercourse set within a cast in-situ concrete wall, whose colour matches the immediately adjacent stonework of McMorran & Whitby's Police Station, screens the ramp to the Police Station. The various changes in level, both on the southern edge as well as on London Wall to the north, are absorbed by staircases, ramps and an elevator. A wide passage, which could host a cafe, beneath the high-rise creates a secure public space overseen round the clock by the receptionist and security personnel in the high-rise's lobby. Street, passage, square, ramps, stairs and raised walkways are resolved into a coherent urban tissue.

In the reception, besides a set of sculptural furnishings and light fittings that appear to surf across the double-height space, two kinds of fabrics; one on 12 panels of enamelled metal wires, the other hand-knotted rugs with the subtle radial inscriptions reminiscent of the Ryoanji Stone Garden, reiterate the building's theme. Even the board marks of the concrete wall behind the wall-hangings were carefully detailed to interact with the visual effect of the sheen of the wire weaving.

30 Finsbury Square and 5 Aldermanbury Square could not be further apart if one were to view the latter from the vantage point of integral exoskeletal structural behaviour. However, the latter office building authoritatively occupies the territory of Semper's principle of cladding. The composition of the cladding elements and the treatment of the material are such that they reinforce this principle: there is not the least pretence that the visible parts are structurally active, for the joints and the separation from the main volume of the building are too distinct. In this high-rise, EPA have realised the corporeality of the cladding system as a screen with an almost ethereal presence.

[1] Eric Parry, quoted by Elaine Knutt, "Striking in its simplicity", *Building Design*, 13 October 2006, p. 20.

[2] Sullivan, Louis H, "The Tall Office Building Artistically Considered", *Kindergarten Chats and other Writings*, New York, 1918, pp. 202–213. Originally published in *Lippincott's*, March 1896.

[3] Loos, Adolf, competition text in English in *The Architecture of Adolf Loos*, ed. Yehuda Safran and Wilfried Wang, London, 1985, p. 60, quoted in German in *Der Architekt Adolf Loos*, ed. Ludwig Münz and Gustav Künstler, Vienna, 1964, p. 177.

Three London Offices

Most built projects take a cycle of five years from start to finish, several in this volume even longer. By contract the gestation period for an office fit-out is about a tenth of this time and the inter-related cycles of short and long design time spans are important for the rhythm of a design studio's life.

opposite: View from the south west meeting room on the 15th floor. Together with the equivalent 20 person room to the southeast these give a complete panorama across the City of London and Westminster and beyond to Southwark.

right: Floor layouts for the 16th, 15th and 14th floors of 5 Aldermanbury Square. View on page 158 is from the reception on the middle floor (15th) looking southwards to Tate Modern. The spiral stair interconnects the three floors.

A fit-out lies somewhere between the impermanence of a film set or exhibition design and the life-cycle of a building. As a type they are prone to being altered or destroyed and it comes as a shock to be asked to design a space a second time, stripped of the walls, finishes and furniture that had seemed so confident. The shock is obviously a remorse about the waste of energy and material as these commissions are often carried out under intense time pressure but also because of the fragmentation under economic or other strains of the complex social bonds of an organisation.

Babcock & Brown

The four floors taken by Babcock & Brown at 5 Aldermanbury Square are centred in plan and section on their reception on the 15th floor. A rectangular space 9.5 m wide x 25 m draws you from the lift lobby, which is characterised as part of the base building, to the spectacular views southwards with the distant focus of Tate Modern's chimney and lightbox. Stripping the space to its metal structure with a series of key movements was intended to suggest a film studio evoking the work of Ken Adams for the original James Bond sets.

From time to time this is a gathering space for the 300 staff, more normally it is a waiting space with direct access to the meeting rooms arranged around it. These provide in a variety of sizes space for more than 100 people. A suspended polished stainless steel spiral stair is cored through the floor levels and literally connects the company. The remaining three floors are arranged in a generous open plan format which replaced the cellular planning of the company's previous office buildings. The external structure of the building envelope provides a robust framework that allows a very flexible plan layout internally.

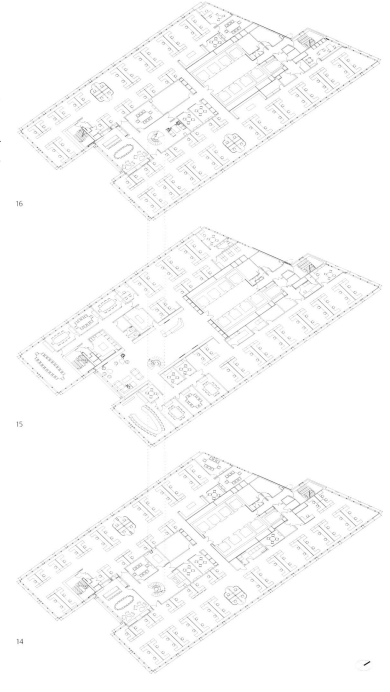

Third floor Grosvenor Street. This is the fourth office in a different building for one developer client, a short term lease in a very restricted floorplan and tight floor to ceiling heights. Monochromatic with the exception of seating fabric and pictures, the optimism of placemaking was evoked through black and white photography digitally printed at the scale of wall panels.

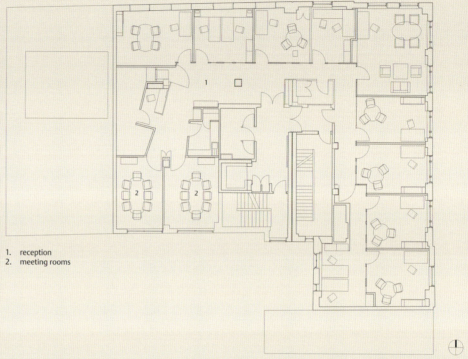

1. reception
2. meeting rooms

Stanhope Plc

Over a period of 20 years Eric Parry Architects has followed one client through four office relocations with items of furniture and pictures becoming the thread of continuity through the complex web of the organisational and building management metamorphosis.

left: View of the meeting rooms from reception.

above: Reception desk with roof landscape playground at the Unite d'Habitation iconic photograph of c. 1952 by Lucien Hervé (opposite).

The fourth floor of Norfolk House in Berkeley Square was the third fit-out for developer/manager Stanhope, a name behind many of the most prominent London schemes from the mid-1980s onwards.

top left:
Corridor to meeting rooms. Inflected veneered wall panels contain the door trimmed with an aluminium flat which holds the glass wall panels.

bottom left:
With bespoke furniture, rug and painted mdf fins, an awkward geometry in plan with a view to a dismal inner court is turned into a dynamic waiting space at the busiest point in the office.

right:
The third setting for the pictures and furniture over a 20 year span.

opposite: Babcock & Brown. View from the crossing, meeting rooms beyond, waiting area to the right, interconnecting suspended stair rising to the 16th floor and descending to the 14th and 13th. Purpose made pressed aluminium panels backed in felt provide acoustic absorption to the otherwise hard surfaces of the studio reception.

St Martin-in-the-Fields

Building at the heart of Westminster is a remarkable achievement. The density of institutions involved in reviewing and approving a design, regardless of the public scrutiny and the interception by pressure groups, self-appointed or otherwise, is daunting. Combining this with the density of the context with the immediate neighbours, their significances and their wardens, as well as the wider architectural discourse, makes for a testing contemporary practice. Architects without the necessary intellectual, psychological and physical constitution may succeed through styling, catchy phrases and stout drinking, but the resultant building will just be another set of the emperor's new clothes.

opposite: View of the Church from New Zealand House along Nash's intended vista from the Mall.

left: Gibbs' church completed in 1726 was a monumental insertion into the essentially Medieval fabric along St Martin's Lane. The coloured shading denotes burial grounds.

centre: In conceiving Trafalgar Square and the new block structure surrounding the Church, Nash created a radically new and complete setting for the church, including the redefined subterranean burial vaults.

right: The competition idea, to redefine the church yard and increase the width of the public route east–west along Church Path providing an entry pavilion and its inverse, a lightwell, as two urban punctuation marks.

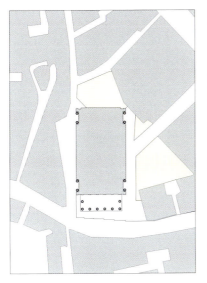
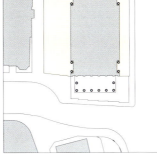
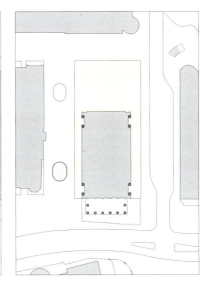

Eighteenth century—Gibbs' church   Nineteenth century—Nash's scheme   Twenty-first century—as proposed

Building at the heart of the City of Westminster, on Trafalgar Square, is symbolic of having arrived at the heart of English culture, especially when the subject is the most laden of all of the sites on the square, James Gibbs' St Martin-in-the-Fields, 1721–1726, and its adjacent former churchyard, vicarage, vestry, school, homeless shelter community centre and public passage (Church Path). Eric Parry Architects were chosen in early 2002 following an international two stage competition in 2001 by the Church of England on the advice from CABE to completely reorganise the site, renovate the interior of the church, oversee a conservation programme for the church's exterior, improve the facilities for the religious and immigrant community, for the social workers and for tourists.

Located at the junction between some of the most intensively frequented tourist destinations, the political and representational centres (parliament and Buckingham Palace), Club Land (both the clubs for established members as well as the nightlife scene), entertainment facilities, Trafalgar Square as the key location for political discourse, South Africa House, and the backstages of life, the vicars of St Martin-in-the-Fields have, since the 1980s, been amongst the most radical in redefining the mission of the contemporary Christian church. The parish has focused on homeless people of all backgrounds, immigrants, tourists, political dissenters, well-meaning Middle-Englanders just in search for a "cuppa" in their arch-parish,

music lovers and all those simply seeking shelter amidst a sea of hyperactivity. In many ways, all of these have some mouthpiece to make themselves heard in any alteration proposal to the "mother ship" of all churches (it also happens to be the royal parish church, as well as that of the admiralty and 10 Downing Street).

Preliminary consultation was undertaken between clients and architects on the one hand and the Diocese's Advisory Committee, Westminster City Council, CABE and English Heritage so as to provide a clear approach to other heritage lobbyists. The previous pattern of use, particularly of the Church's crypt and the annex to the north of the church, included the usual decades of makeshift alterations, well-intentioned interior decoration, technically degraded installations and tacky tack-ons, each with their constituency of sentimental admirers. However, the entire collection of spaces made for an undignified environment that was tolerated by most users as a result of numbing familiarity. Much of the external stonework, covered by soot and grime, had been degraded by decades of neglect and acid rain.

By the spring of 2003, EPA's initial proposals for the revitalisation of the church were supported by all of the aforementioned institutions including the Prince's Foundation and the Georgian Society. By widening Church Path between the church and the annex buildings to the north, for the first time the two contextual components have been brought

top left: Churchyard at the east end of the site with York stone paving on the brick burial vaults built to John Nash's design of 1829. The removal of the market was a difficult decision, but justified by the rebalancing of uses across the site as a whole.

top right, middle and below left and right: A sequence of photographs by Chris Steele-Perkins documenting the work of care at St Martin-in-the-Fields in the existing fabric, 2002.
—Entrance to the night shelter via steps adjacent to the northwest vestibule of the church (ref plans of the existing fabric p. 170)
—Reception to the night shelter
—Night shelter rest room with clients artwork displayed on the wall
—Multipurpose day room here used as art room, in the old school classroom.

middle left: The church interior with remnants of the polychromatic decorative scheme paid for by Harrod's to mark Queen Victoria's Diamond Jubilee. Just evident are the fixed choir stalls and the east end configuration which will change to a more flexible arrangement closer to the original Gibbs' scheme.

existing ground floor

1. Austen Williams Room
2. George Richards Room
3. vestry hall
4. kitchen
5. boiler
6. care kitchen
7. care reception
8. care day room
9. consultation
10. church path
11. vestry
12. churchyard
13. care entry
14. vestibule
15. portico
16. green room
17. crypt entrance
18. side altar
19. vergers

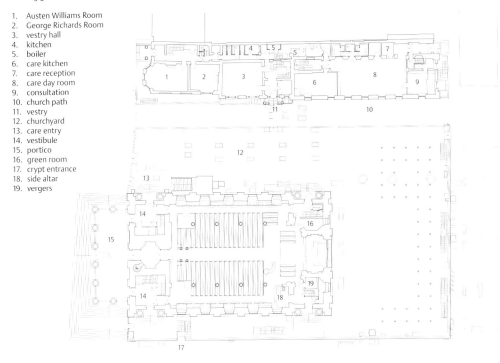

existing lower ground floor/crypt level

1. care office
2. care advice
3. office
4. laundry
5. consultation
6. kitchen
7. care staff
8. care activites
9. art room
10. music room
11. loveday room
12. Ho Ming Wah Centre
13. care waiting
14. cafe
15. crypt entrance
16. brass rubbing centre
17. shop
18. gallery
19. boiler
20. Dick Sheppard Chapel
21. workshop
22. store

1:750

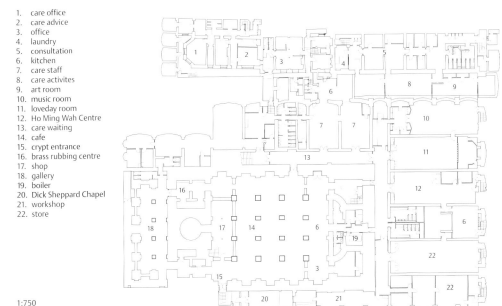

into public consciousness by two small architectural interventions: a generous lightwell bringing daylight into the northeastern segment of the newly organised two levels of underground spaces and a glass entrance pavilion (the idea behind these two elements parallels Eric Parry's rug design for the lobby of 5 Aldermanbury Square).

EPA's design is the second largest urban and architectural intervention in this dense part of London since John Nash changed the character of this area from a Medieval street pattern to a nineteenth century representational fabric. In 1826 Nash rendered the church an object through the construction of Trafalgar Square, the removal of the Royal Mews and the widening of surrounding streets and the addition of the so-called North Range facing Church Path. This time, nearly two centuries later, the ever-increasing additional activities initiated by the church since World War II, necessitate reoccupying the North Range as well as being housed in the two levels of basements beneath the widened Church Path and the former churchyard. In many ways, the relationship of the church proper—the nave—to the ancillary program resembles the increasing dilemma between the ancillary spaces and auditoria of nineteenth and twentieth century theatres. Here at St Martin-in-the-Fields, most of the ancillary activities are not represented through architecture above ground; they are just adjacent to various forms of lightwells. Thus, beneath the newly formed churchyard and the widened Church Path four meeting areas have been located: the church hall, a chapel, the Ho Ming Wah Chinese community centre and a music rehearsal room.

Wherever possible, EPA have added floor surface by inserting new levels. For example, the homeless shelter. The Connection benefits from a simplified circulation system above where some new rooms are included and the reorganisation of tall spaces such as the roof void for extra administration space.

below: Isometric projection of the redefined public realm above and below ground. Apart from the architectural and spatial resolution one of the goals of the competition scheme was to clarify the entrances to the dense mix of social groupings using the site.

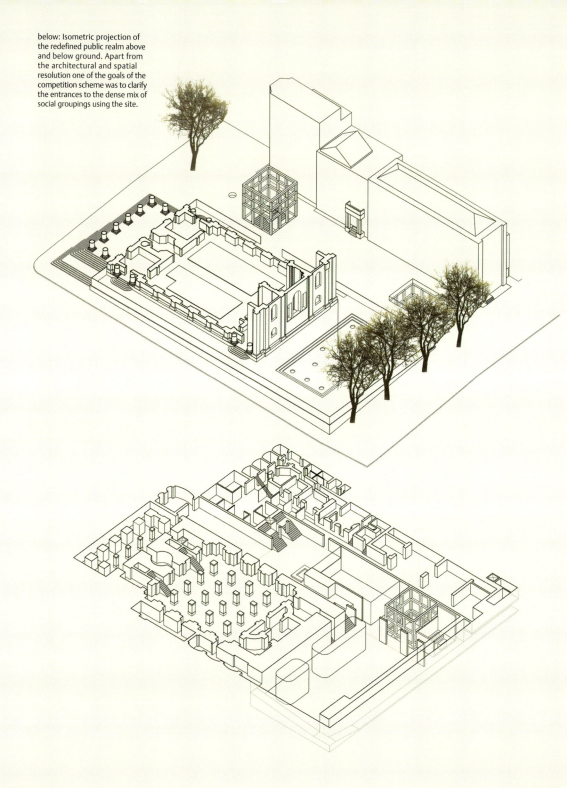

opposite: Three views from the competition submission.

top: Across Trafalgar Square, new entrance pavilion modestly visible

middle: Walking westwards towards the new entrance pavilion along the widened Church Path.

bottom: Looking up from the lightwell, a new perspective of the church from the proposed subterranean cloister.

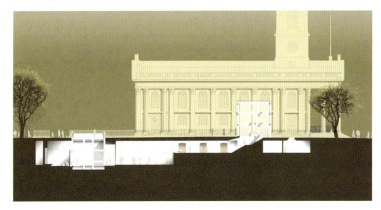

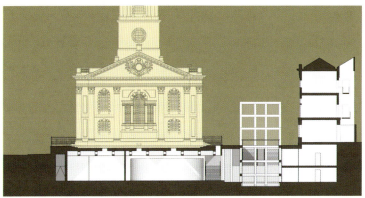

This page and the facing page: Drawings and model photographs from the architectural competition submission January 2002.

top left and right: Photographs of the model from west left, and southeast right.

middle left: Section east–west through the raised pavilion and its inverse lowered lightwell along Church Path.

bottom left: Section south–north through the churchyard, lightwell and the North Range.

proposed ground floor

1. Austen Williams Room
2. vestry hall
3. reception
4. day room
5. pavilion
6. church
7. lightwell
8. new gates
9. vestibule with new lift and stair to crypt
10. redefined churchyard
11. portico
12. ramped access to church

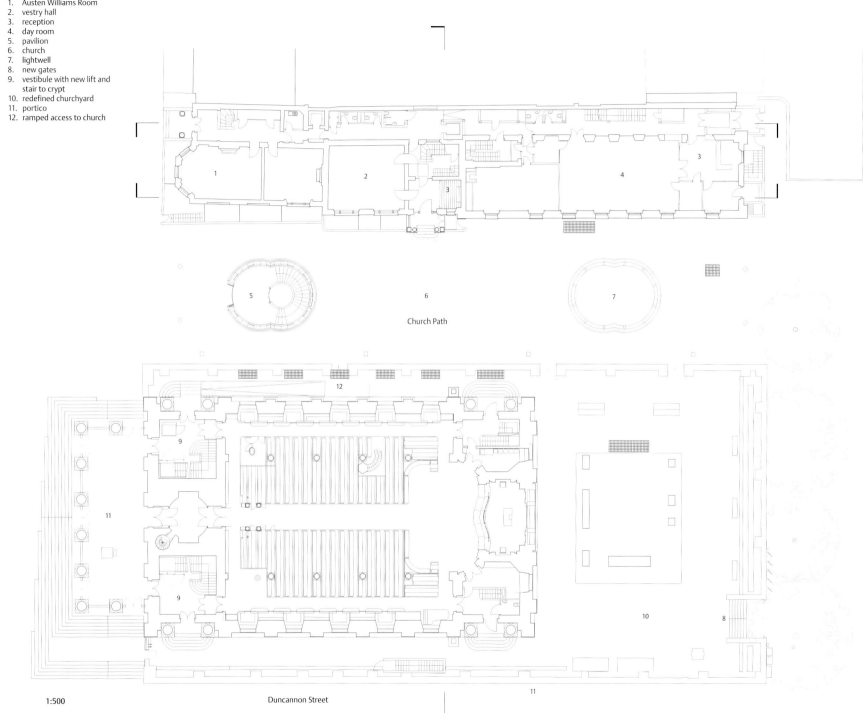

1:500

Church Path

Duncannon Street

proposed lower ground/crypt level

1. care activity
2. dining room
3. medical room
4. laundry
5. refuse
6. exhibition and display
7. tickets
8. shop
9. gallery
10. cafe
11. kitchen
12. office
13. changing room

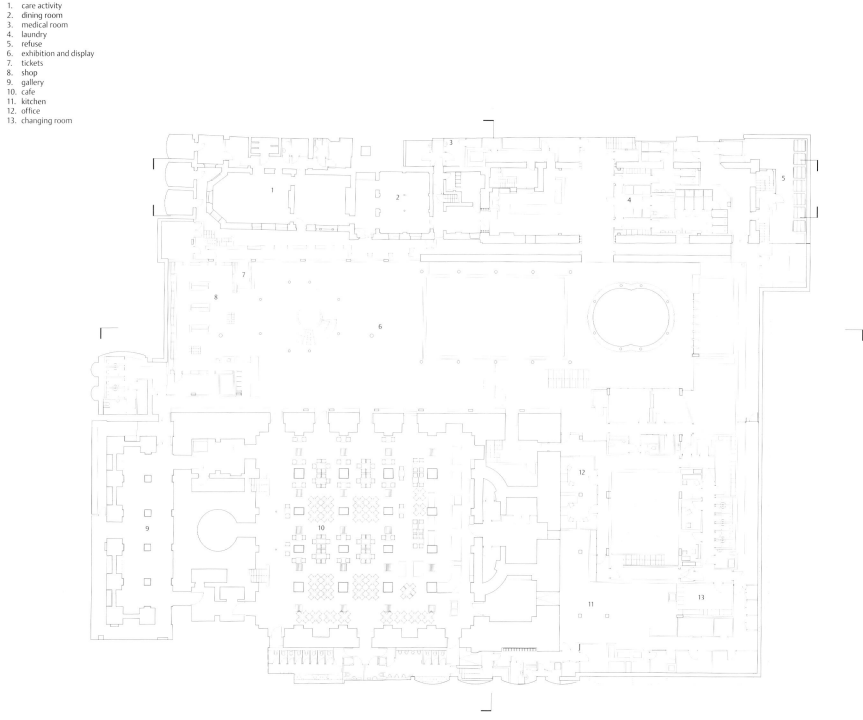

proposed basement level

1. plant room
2. parish kitchen
3. store
4. church hall
5. cloister
6. lightwell
7. chapel
8. Ho Ming Wah Centre
9. office
10. music rehearsal room
11. kitchen

opposite: Drawing from April 2003, exploring the scale of the new pavilion between Gibbs' stonework and Nash's painted render facades. Materials envisaged for the pavilion are granite plinth with stacked low-ion glass walls and shot-peened stainless steel roof.

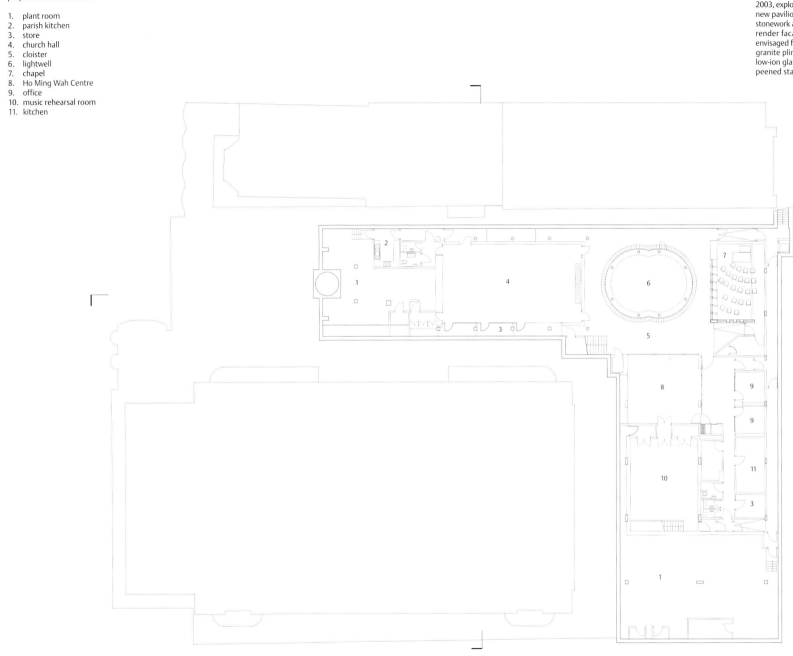

1:500

below: Section south–north looking west. Below the body of the restored church the crypt is connected to the new public space defined in height by the structure and rainwater drainage at pavement level and the crypt floor level. A new 3.3 metre wide building to the rear of the north range is a crucial new addition to allow circulation, additional smaller rooms and parts of the servicing strategy for the whole site.

opposite left: Sketch study of the Dick Sheppard chapel including proposals for the altar, tapestry, benches and wall mounted candle holders.

opposite right: Preliminary sketch of the lightwell and interlocking circular form.

The fact that there is over double the quantity of floor area available at basement levels, and a marked improvement in the quality of the architecture, is a vote of thanks for the parish work carried out by St Martin-in-the-Fields in the last decades.

For St Martin-in-the-Fields itself, EPA will be able to remove the accretions of dirt and circumstantial embellishment in terms of lighting, painting or furnishings and by judicious selection of glass for windows, luminaries, colours and paints. This together with the re-positioning of for example the pulpit will clarify the church's interior. The old Baroque steps to the sanctuary will be set free; a pendant pair of benches will be placed to define a multi-purpose space in front of the sanctuary (for music performances, readings, etc.). An elevator will be carefully and unobtrusively included. Significantly, and with equal subtlety (and one hopes that the future users will appreciate the difference) the old lino floor in the nave will be replaced with real Purbeck stone. Corporeality in the wider sense has to do with the lasting and credible instantiation of an idea. Architecture, when judiciously realised, can help to assert this.

As to the wider role of architecture in this scheme, EPA's insertion not only of the underground program, but also of the two objects based on two intersecting circles of the same radius, the one an object, the other a void, within the carefully proportioned public space, condenses

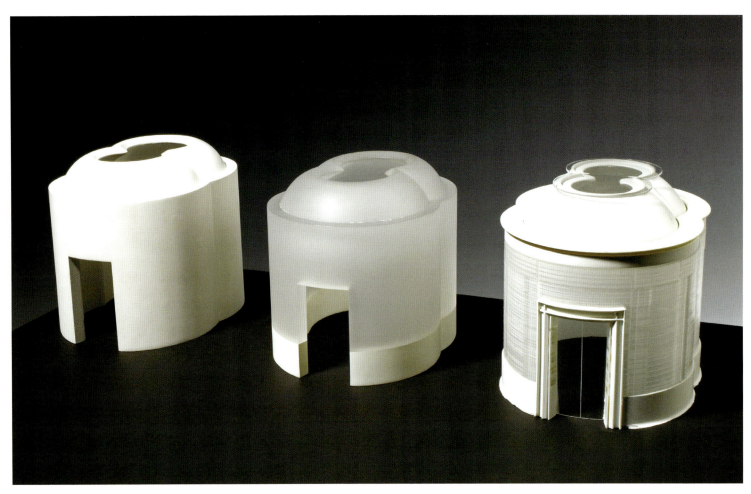

left: The three stages of material development of the pavilion design. Solid monolithic form; stone plinth and resin wall and stainless steel roof (shot-peened exterior, polished soffit internally). Following technical and cost considerations a compromised fourth solution of scribed structural glass panels was developed and happily dropped in favour of the fifth solution: a double skinned structurally glazed wall with a light reflective interlayer.

below: Study of the pavilion with structured reflective glass panels, 2007.

opposite; Pencil study of the stacked glass pavilion viewed from St Martin's Place between the North Range and the Church, 2003.

significant precedents such as market halls of middle England (for example Yarn Market in Dunster) that are set at the centre of wide public spaces, or the more enclosed Donato Bramante's Tempietto of San Pietro in Montorio on the outskirts of Rome, c. 1502, and Gibbs' Radcliffe Camera in Oxford, 1737–1749. The glass entrance pavilion at St Martin-in-the-Fields will subtly find its place and maximise its physical presence by its unavoidable proximity to passers-by. The density of the glass, the refraction of light and shapes will give the passer-by an enticing impression of an optic aureola. In its compositional detail it is treated like a pilastered tempietto, a solid glass porch, echoing the entrance porch to the National Portrait Gallery on the other side of the street. The cupola to the pavilion with its glazed oculus will terminate the volume of intersecting circular walls in a Baroque manner. The careful profiling of the oculus will ensure the gradation of daylight around the edges without sharp shadows; its profile suggesting the obverse of an Attic acrocup.

proposed mezzanine level

1. consultation / office
2. office / store

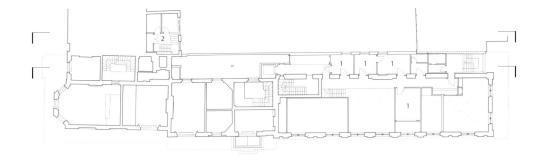

proposed first floor

1. clergy office
2. vicar's study
3. office reception
4. it training room
5. hub / training area
6. teaching room
7. art room
8. it office
9. consultation room
10. clergy flat

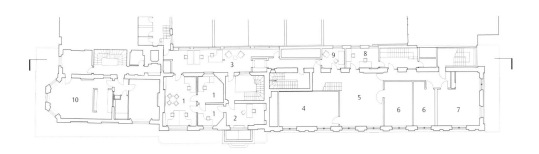

sections

1. consultation room / office
2. entrance hall
3. store
4. office reception
5. office
6. staff room
7. office
8. medical room
9. kitchenette
10. clergy flat

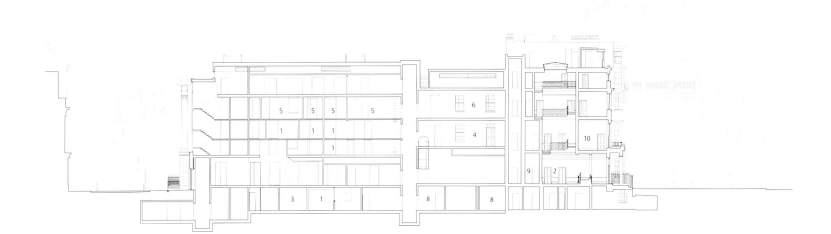

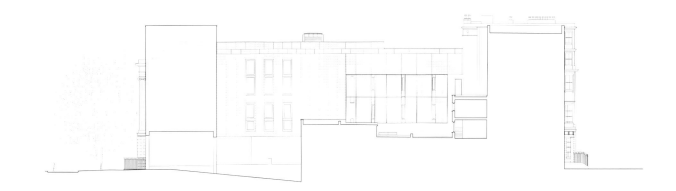

The pavilion's counterpart, the lightwell, has a profiled balustrade that renders the void volume into a simple high vase. Together with the stainless steel handrail, the edge of the opening is given a form that is worlds apart from the voided modernist abstraction so prevalent even in nearby cultural edifices. Minimal abstraction, that ideal aesthetic status of deracinated modernism, would render a balustrade in laminated sheet glass fixed to a concrete base with a stainless steel plate; as if to say: "look, no hands" but actually meaning, "look, no grounding in the evolution of form, no culture".

Architectural discourse had been in this state before right here at St Martin-in-the-Fields. Gibbs, author of a recipe architectural treatise and designer of the Radcliffe Camera in Oxford, undoubtedly his greatest achievement, created a much-copied icon with the church for St Martin-in-the-Fields.[2] As widely as it was copied, it is nevertheless an unresolved attempt at superimposing the Gothic originated steeple directly on the ridge of the roof of a neo-Classical temple, a temple that moreover just slightly reduces the width of the hexastyle pedimented porch in comparison to the main body of the church. There is no representation on the principal facades as to the structural weight of the tower, no mediation at the roof between the walls of the steeple and the inclination of the roof, in short, no conceptual-compositional correction to an issue of architectural culture. Gibbs' earlier St Mary-le-Strand, 1714–1723, while of a more modest size, does integrate steeple with nave. Gibbs' contemporary, Nicholas Hawksmoor, on the other hand designed a handful of churches, each of them brilliant studies in the compositional reconciliation of Gothic steeple typology and neo-Classical temple (for example, St Mary Woolnoth of 1711–1716, Christ Church Spitalfields of 1714–1729, St George's Bloomsbury of 1716–1731).

Gibbs' St Martin-in-the-Fields represents an early success of the mechanical composition of architectural elements without recourse to the necessary adaptation or transformation of compositional rules to resolve new cultural problems. If, in typological terms, temples previously were not compromised by the imposition of steeples, then how would architectural design principles have to change to accommodate this? Hawksmoor's three cited churches provide a spectrum of choices in which the compositional challenge is resolved in a cultured way.

EPA's two very small architectural statements—the entrance pavilion and the lightwell—are milestones in the insistence on the rootedness of culture without which much of what we do, whether architects or not, becomes just a relationless utterance. The density of references embedded in the two main architectural statements embraces wider worlds than personal aesthetic preferences of an individual architect. The renovated and amplified St Martin-in-the-Fields is one of the few examples of a piece of architecture, in which the role of space, whether public or interior, is granted dominance over form, and where, when form is called to the stage, it speaks with precision in detail and depth of meaning.

[1] Recalling the Vesica Piscis of traditional Christian art and the geometric construction of the arch in Islamic architecture. A potential reference to ancient Chinese philosophical concept of Yin—Yang, heaven and earth, male and female, etc..

[2] James Gibbs, Rules for Drawing the Several Parts of Architecture in a more exact and easy manner than has been heretofore practised by which all fractions, in dividing the principal members and their parts, are avoided, London 1732. This treatise became an influential handbook in English speaking countries.

Projects Summary

Old Wardour House

Situated beside the historic Old Wardour Castle, built in the late fourteenth century, Old Wardour House has a rich history. Major alterations have been made to some or all of the buildings on this site in the 1690s, 1740s, 1870s, 1900s and 1960s, leaving a distinctive, eclectic, traceable pattern.

A number of readjustments to the house together with the new extension reflect a changing domestic circumstance from one of a family supported by employed staff, with the laundry and kitchen embedded in the plan, to the self sufficiency of a family where, for instance, cooking and eating are a shared and less socially hierarchical.

The openness of the new extension is both a response to a brief to allow more light into the house, ringed as it is by hills and woods, and to the adjacent sixteenth century ruins of domestic walls with their very fine masonry. The extension was built for £170k with Luke Hughes, the co-owner, taking on the general contracting.

C: Luke Hughes
M&E: Max Fordham
SE: Michael Hadi Associates
QS: EPA
A: EP LN*1 TP*2 YK BB
Date: 1990–2005

Wimbledon School of Art

The new building provides at ground floor studio space, exhibition space, cafe and above a new presentation, criticism and lecture space. The building forms one side of a new court garden and Adams Kara Taylor's elegant steel structure allows the ground flood to be opened up to form one continuous space when needed. The upper space is designed to be used for experimental work including sound and light installations and is acoustically isolated. The graded chromatic brick wall was the first time that we had used ceramic as part of the external fabric of a building.

C: Wimbledon School of Art
M&E: Michael Popper Associates
SE: Adams Kara Taylor
QS: AJP Frankham
EPA Team: EP JD*2 DK*1 RC
Date: 1997–2004

Royal Lancaster Hotel

This project is a reminder to the fact that from unpromising beginnings a project can, with skill and care, deliver a huge benefit both internally but also, as here, to the public realm. Following a planning permission in 2000 (Volume 1), detailed design commenced in 2002. The works comprised clearing away 1980s glass extensions and streamlining the frontage with a new stone facade. A white Spanish limestone was used in conjunction with large glazed panels set in polished, stainless-steel frames to create a new self-supporting urbane skin for the hotel. The length of continuous wall is 208 m long interrupted for now by the section shared with London Underground, a memorial to the grinding complexity of the organisation. The renewal enabled the extension of the building line to the site boundary in two places, and as a result the hotel offer was expanded to include 12 syndicate rooms, hotel offices, the Island restaurant and private dining rooms. Our work is not be confused with the earlier entrance and canopy.

C: Landmark Hotel Group
M&E: Leonard Engineering
SE: Bolton Priestley
QS: GBP Fitzsimon
A: EP NL NM* JO, PF RC LME
Date: 1997–2004

30 Finsbury Square

The development of this project to planning permission has been described in EPA Volume 1 and in this volume the built project is recorded. The design evolved from a study of the urban setting, including the use of the public square. The project creates an optimal internal office arrangement for flexible office use with no internal columns. The elevations are a unique system developed for the project with load bearing limestone piers supporting the internal steel beams. The depth of the facade provides additional solar shading which asserts the energy conservation strategy.

The building has won an RIBA award, AIA/UK Design Excellence Award, a commendation from the British Council for Offices, and was on the short-list for the Stirling Prize 2003.

C: Scottish Widows plc
DM: Jones Lang LaSalle
M&E: Hilson Moran Partnership
SE: Whitbybird
QS: Gardiner & Theobald
A: EP RK*1 NJ*2 MC SM NM JL ML PC TT
Date: 1999–2002

London Residence

The first site visit to a Victorian villa was in 1999. It had faux Rococo interiors and an overgrown garden reminiscent of a Hitchcock movie set which had to be balanced against our client's ambition to create an important contemporary London family house. The idea was to embrace the vertically ordered villa to its garden side and flank and rear by a single storey enfilade of north-facing rooms with a frameless wall of glass creating continuity with the landscaped terraces designed by Christopher Bradley-Hole. An impressive marble-clad subterranean spa lies below the garden terrace and is lit by a glass oculus.

C: Private Client
M&E: Michael Popper Associates
SE: Adams Kara Taylor
QS: Davis Langdon
LA: Christopher Bradley-Hole
A: EP JSA* JS RB RC DK
Date: 1999–2002

10 Paternoster Square

I was asked by Stuart Lipton on 11 December 1999 whether I could help with an unspecified project and the next day drawings of the site and previous proposals arrived. By the 19 December the first design review took place at the offices of Stanhope. I had up to that point taken a peripheral interest in the tumultuous history of the Paternoster Square development. This project is the most prominent building within Sir William Whitfield's masterplan for the new square, a difficult trapezoidal site plan bisected by St Paul's heights in section. The London Stock Exchange chose to occupy the building over reputedly 40 other new city properties. Whilst we led the design and detailing of the building, Sheppard Robson were appointed to lead the documentation. A joint team was formed in an annex to their Camden offices and Nigel Lea moved there for the duration of the project.

C: Mitsubishi Estates
M&E: Waterman Gore
SE: Waterman Partnership
QS: Davis Langdon
A: EP RK NL* SW RB MC
Date: 1999–2003

Bedford Library

We won the RIBA organised competition to design a new library building for Bedford School in October 2000. The site for the new library is on a former car park to the west of the existing outmoded school library. The library addresses the range of main school buildings. A sequence of spaces within progress from the low lobby housing the newspapers and journals, through to the expansive study and bookstall areas facing the garden. From a single front elevation the building splits into two barrel vaulted wings. The quality of this finely constructed library is not evident from photographs and is an example of a building that needs to be experienced to be understood.

C: Bedford School
M&E: Michael Popper Associates
SE: Adams Kara Taylor
QS: Davis Langdon
A: EP SW* PC NL NA
Date: 2001–2003

Gresham Street

Following a successful planning consent for 54–66 Gresham Street and 25 Old Jewry the client acquired 26 Old Jewry and 13 Ironmonger Lane. These properties had been the headquarters of the City of London Police around a listed eighteenth century core within a brick facade. The design takes two awkward and inefficient office building and creates one building that worked with the retained and listed core and facade while creating a contemporary interpretation of the particular quality of the City's monumental classical buildings. The site was sold once planning permission was granted and taken forward by architects who copied much of the elevation detail whilst drastically diluting the material intention. It is always disappointing to turn the corner to recognise a likeness of a friend without the personality.

C: Frogmore Investments
M&E: Hilson Moran Partnership
SE: Adams Kara Taylor
QS: Barrie Tankel Partnership
A: EP NJ RB* LN
Date: 2000–2004

Turner Contemporary Margate

We were one of six teams shortlisted for the ill fated first competition won by Snohetta/Spence for their 'pebble in the sea' proposal. I have a vivid memory of an eminent curator viewing the exhibited proposals with as much suspicion as I felt. Now I look at the project being built and know that it is strikingly close in siting, massing and material to our proposal and feel a deep irritation with the misguided judging process. The building was conceived as a white sculptural form, which also reflected the tradition of working seaside buildings and covered open spaces. The external walls were to be made of in-situ concrete clad in a skin of glass to protect and reflect the atmosphere. The submission included an urban scaled model and pastel drawings of the main elevations reflecting diurnal and landscape differences.

C: Turner Contemporary
A: EP RK PF JO
Date: 2001

23 Savile Row

The brief was to replace Fortress House, the Headquarters of English Heritage, a familiar landmark building originally constructed on bomb damaged land as a headquarters building for a nationalised industry after World War II. There were several early design iterations. Caught between the politics of taste in Westminster and the desires of the owners to maximise the development opportunity, the design, engineering and crafting of the elevations in particular represent a hard won struggle. The resulting wall section incorporates string courses for the first time. My choice of Joel Shapiro as a collaborator and the fertile five year dialogue that ensued was through a deep empathy for his work and the liberation it has brought to the tautness of the architecture.

C: Legal & General (prior to construction) D2 Private
M&E / SE: Arup
QS: AYH Arcadis - Mott Green Wall
A: EP RB* RK BH MR BD GC DC ER ZF LN FE AVO NH
Date: 2001–ongoing

5 Aldermanbury Square

I had three key meetings with Peter Rees, the chief planning officer, during the design of the height and massing of the building. The first established that the building was to stand alone sitting, as it does, above the crossing of the Roman fort rather than bound by a common cornice as seen opposite in the Foster and Rogers buildings on Wood Street. Our model bears the pencil marks from this dialogue. At the second the question of material was explored with Peter Rees mooting a preference for a metal and glass building. At the third the architectural order and quality was agreed by a detail drawing and a standard of material ambition—a David Mellor stainless steel spoon. The new 18-storey building raised above the public space consists of two staggered wings divided by a receding central section that admits light into the triple-height ground floor reception space. The facades are formed in stainless steel cladding enclosing all perimeter structure within a double height arrangement. The building was shortlisted for the Stirling Prize in 2009.

C: Scottish Widows plc & American Teachers Fund
DM: Hanover Cube
M&E: Hilson Moran Partnership
SE: Whitbybird
QS: Northcroft
A: EP NJ* JS TP MC NH YK RL SBU NM FE
Date: 2001–2007

Norfolk House

Completed in 2002, this is the third of three office fit-outs for Stanhope Properties. The first was a 20,000ft² at Lansdowne House, Berkeley Square in 1998, the second, smaller offices at Mount Row were completed in 1996 and the latest is Norfolk House, St James' Square. The floor is divided into meeting rooms overlooking the square and an open plan office. Between the circulation is formed as a gallery for the company's art collection.

C: Stanhope
M&E / SE: Arup
QS: Davis Langdon & Everest
A: EP, RK, NM*
Date: 2002

Royal Garden Clubhouse Shanghai

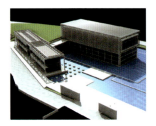

The new clubhouse provides the principal amenity for the Royal Garden residential development in Shanghai. A two-storey building that appears to float out over a lake, above a swimming pool whose sides lift up in the summer providing bathers access to the lake in fine weather. The upper floor provides a state of the art gymnasium, a multipurpose fitness room and refreshment and meeting area. The hall is connected to an buried element housing leisure and sports facilities including a spa, massage rooms, basketball courts, a crèche, offices, games rooms, a car park, plant rooms and a large foyer providing the social hub to the clubhouse. A retail building on two storeys provides a restaurant, health clinic and shops.

C: Yanfull Corporation
M&E / SE / QS: Shanghai Haipo Architectural Design Co. Ltd
A: EP JS* NM NA
Date: 2001–2003

Bedford Music School

We won an architectural competition, the second for this school, in 2003. The new Music School, with a construction budget of £2.1 million, was built on the site of an existing house used as a music school, to the south of the listed school chapel erected by JF Bodley in 1908. The Music School is a complex of Recital Hall and practice rooms which are connected by the glazed street to the teaching wing. The Recital Hall, designed to seat up to 140, faces the playing fields, with an elevation of alternating large scaled glass and stainless steel panels. These create a play between interior and exterior and were an important step in the development of the use of metal and glass in our subsequent projects, particularly Aldermanbury Square and St Martin-in-the-Fields. Completed at the end of 2005, the building was opened by Sir Peter Maxwell Davies.

C: Bedford School
M&E: White Young Green (preceded by Max Fordham at competition stage)
SE: Adams Kara Taylor
QS: Davis Langdon
Acoustic: Paul Gillieron Acoustic Design
A: EP NL PC* NA NH JD YK LME
Date: 2002–2005

St Martin-in-the-Fields

The project was the subject of a two-stage competition with over three hundred submissions of interest in 2001. Winning this competition, our most public commission to date, was obviously highly significant. At the first site visit both the extent and the state of decay of the fabric was clear and not just of the church; for instance the Nash burial vaults designed for the dead were being used intensively by the living. The proposals include the refurbishment and conservation of Gibbs' Grade I listed church and crypt, the reconstruction of all the subterranean spaces, the rationalisation and extension of the Grade II listed Nash terrace to the north and the reordering of the public spaces above ground taking heed of the positive consequences of the World Squares for All project then unbuilt. Planning permission was granted after an inevitably complex process in October 2003 and fundraising for the £36 million continued following a Heritage Lottery grant of £14.7 million leaving a daunting shortfall for a parish church to raise.

C: St Martin-in-the-Fields
M&E: Max Fordham & partners
SE: Alan Baxter & Associates
QS: Gardiner & Theobald
A: EP RK* TL CB LN SM JP RC NA NL SBU FP JD GC OW GH BB JO LME TO AM
Date: 2002–ongoing

Iringan Hijau Apartments

While Damai Suria (Volume 1) was being constructed our client commissioned a second scheme on a nearby site within the same three-storey planning zone. Planning permission was granted, but the development was put on hold during the regional financial crisis. In 2002 work recommenced only for the planners to rezone the area to ten storeys. After designing a proposal at ten storeys the policy reverted back to the three. The current scheme is materially interesting with an in-situ base rising to white rendered walls. The generosity of scale and space is only the preserve of the super rich in denser cities like London, Hong Kong or New York. The common landscape is likewise generous creating shade from the sun and shelter from the tropical rain. The long gestation is reflected in the refinement of the composition of the elevations and section.

C: Dawntree Properties
M&E / SE: Arup
QS: Davis Langdon & Seah
EPA Team: EP NJ LN* GC PC
Local arch: C'arch
Date: 2002–ongoing

Holburne Museum of Art, Bath

When the Holburne Museum was created in 1916 from the shell of the 1795 garden entrance building it closed itself off with an exedral garden wall and a stair that severed the axis with Great Pulteney Street, one of the most impressive eighteenth century streets in Europe. The proposal aims to add exhibition, archive, education and cafe space will restore the Janus headed character of the original and hopefully lead once more to the close integration of the town and Sydney Gardens. Change to a Grade I listed building in a UNESCO World Heritage Site was bound to stir opposition but the struggle which began with a council officer's unforgettable taunt 'lose your dream' continues. The use of glazed ceramic and glass was finally accepted and planning permission granted in 2007, six years of continuous effort after the invited competition.

C: Trustees of the Holburne Museum of Art
M&E: Atelier 10
SE: Momentum
QS: Faithful & Gould
EPA Team: EP RB*1 CH*2 CB GP GH TO RL JS
Date: 2002–ongoing

Metropole Building and 10 Whitehall Place

Following a limited competition we were appointed to design a replacement for the Metropole building, a crumbling Bath stone bruiser designed as a four hundred bed hotel and since World War II used as a headquarters for the Royal Navy. As a locally cherished period piece of the urban context of Whitehall it was a difficult design development but the proposed arcuated Portland stone facade and recessed metal fenestration with public access to a rooftop conservatory restaurant overlooking the Thames would have made a fine replacement. Eventually under political pressure the Crown Estate withdrew the application, sold the building which will revert to hotel use, the only reasonable alternative to demolition.

C: Crown Estate
M&E: Waterman Gore
SE: Whitbybird
QS: Northcroft
A: EP NJ RB* YK JD JO RCO
Date: 2002–2005

Timothy Taylor Gallery Dering Street

Timothy Taylor commissioned me to recast the spaces vacated by Anthony D'Offay into his own home. The key to this project was to link the two floors creating a sense of unified space. We did this with a new precast concrete stair. The ground floor is now dedicated to hanging space only whilst the first floor consists of showing rooms, offices, stock room, storage areas, a framing workshop and service rooms. The new screeded ground floor and plain white walls provide a working interior as a background for display whilst the timber boards of the first floor create a more domestic setting. Like switching a light on in a darkened room the gallery spaces are given shape and scale by the art placed in them. The ground floor galleries are analogies to the body, the first floor spaces to the mind, the challenge is to connect them, the third, in summary, poses the challenge of using the poetics of the pavement and of the everyday as a starting point rather than the monumental.

C: Timothy Taylor Gallery
M&E: Michael Hadi Associates
Contractor: Robert McAlpine
A: EP JSA* FP
Date: 2003

Millbank Aberdeenshire

We won an invited competition to create a masterplan for the redevelopment of a settlement at Millbank in Aberdeenshire. The Client, the trustees of an estate, has a long ambition for the development to attract employment to the settlement, improve amenities for the area and provide a mix of dwelling types. The brief required a sustainable community to be created with sustainable domestic architecture, servicing infrastructure and landscape proposals. The masterplan will start modestly but allows for future expansion through a design guide. We worked closely with Aberdeenshire County Council and have coordinated community consultation workshops to integrate the existing community and councillor into the design process. The masterplan proposal locates the Community Hall at its centre creating continuity between the existing community and the new. Outline planning permission was achieved. This is the first masterplanned settlement for rural Scotland in recent years.

C: Cluny Estates
Independent sustainability consultant: Dr Bill Brogden
SE: Alan Baxter & Associates
QS: Baxter Dunn & Grey
LA: Latz und Partner
A: EP JS* YK NA JSC BB
Date: 2003

King's Cross Central

We were invited to submit a design for an office building in the broad wedge of space between King's Cross and St Pancras stations which is being developed by Argent St George. The scheme bounded by the canal is a part of a much larger urban development that will create a new district in London. The footprint of the office buildings has been determined through the masterplan by Allies and Morrison and Porphyrios Associates. Mirroring the site our building has a trapezoidal plan with view northwards to the gasometers and nineteenth century granary warehouse whilst fronting the new Pancras Square. The weathering steel structure of the proposal which is exposed externally, with white ceramic louvers will create shading on the more exposed elevations. The matt rust red and reflective surfaces of glass and ceramic will complement each other and echo the pragmatic but awesome surrounding Victorian architecture and engineering.

C: Argent St George
M&E: J Roger Preston Group
SE: Adams Kara Taylor
QS: Davis Langdon
A: EP NJ* YK
Date: 2003–ongoing

185 Park Street

Following the win of a limited invited competition in April 2003, the practice was commissioned to develop proposals for Chelsfield plc for a 40,000 m² mixed-use development adjacent to Tate Modern in Bankside. The scheme has three separate buildings linked by new public spaces. A triangular residential tower creates a focus to the southwest corner with the smaller brick building behind. The 20,000 m² commercial building has retail and community uses to revitalise the public realm.

C: Motcomb Estates
M&E: Hilson Moran Partnership
SE: Adams Kara Taylor
QS: Gleeds
A: EP NL* TP NH
Date: 2003–on hold

Aldermanbury Square Landscape

The character of the space under the building was emerging when the Corporation of London seized the opportunity to redesign the Aldermanbury Square landscape. This led to a new urban landscape. Under the building south light penetrates the cave-like world of cascading water and the interior of the reception space. The west axis is terminated with 88 Wood Street. The east in the intimate garden which is differentiated in the dense low canopy of esplanade plane trees and light silver birch canopies to the north. It replaced a space deadened by a race track of asphalt to service the building with a central slither of inaccessible garden.

C: The City of London
A: EP NJ JS* NH
Date: 2004–2006

Grosvenor Waterside

Within this St James' residential development we worked with a team of architects on a group of new buildings within the established masterplan. Our almost impossible site of environmental significance was the Thames side basin. To allow views to the river from the northern buildings then under construction, we evolved a concept of four toe-print shaped buildings sitting lightly on concrete tripods and allowing views between. The 60 units were to be accessed from the northwest corner of the basin through a common bridge link.

C: St James
M&E / SE: Arup
QS: Davis Langdon
A: EP RK* CB JSC
Date: 2004

60 Threadneedle Street

We won a competition for a new nine-storey office building in the Bank Conservation area of the City of London in 2004. The previous complex of buildings on the site was completed in 1969 for the London Stock Exchange and consisted of a 26-storey office tower with a four-storey podium of trading floors extending to the west. In 2003 the Stock Exchange relocated, coincidentally to our building on Paternoster Square (pp. 78–79 this volume). This allowed an unrestricted perimeter of 15 m wide lit internally by two rhomboid shaped atria. The dark metal elements of the elevations follow the trabeated principal of previous work but with an emphasis on the horizontal projecting to give solar shading and an urban rhythm to Threadneedle Street. The architecture responds to the corners of many monumental city buildings and most prominently that of the Bank of England.

C: Hammerson
M&E: Hilson Moran Partnership
SE: WSP Cantor Seinuk
QS: Davis Langdon
A: EP NL*1 MC*2 RD TO CT AVO DM JD GC SBU YK BB
Date: 2004–ongoing

Portsmouth Historic Dockyard

We have proposed two alternatives for redeveloping Boathouse 4 within Portsmouth's Historic Dockyard. The first is to create a multi-purpose dining, events and market facility which will occupy the entire building. The second is to create a destination entertainment venue, likely to be operated by a single operator, which will add to the rich diversity of attractions to be found at the Dockyard. Both proposals will integrate this historically very interesting building within its broader context and bring it back to life, providing a first class events and tourist facility at such a pivotal location in the Dockyard.

C: Portsmouth Naval Property Trust
A: EP JS* YK
Date: 2004–ongoing

50 New Bond Street 14 St George Street

This is our third project for Scottish Widows who own much of this greater urban block. Attempts by others have been made for more than a decade to make sense of the run-down properties. The current solution to re-build and refurbish a 90 m long by 30 m wide urban site with mixed uses incorporating two new office buildings with new elevations to New Bond and Maddox Street with retail uses at ground floor and in a large new unit in New Bond Street, is very interesting as an approach to both urban design and building design. The synthesis of parts will be reinforced by two art commissions, the lighting of the faience of New Bond Street by Martin Richman and a mosaic soffit to the Maddox Street elevation by Antoni Malinonski.

C: Scottish Widows plc
DM: Hanover Cube
M&E: Hilson Moran Partnership
SE: Ramboll UK
QS: Gardiner & Theobald
A: EP NJ*(1) JS*(2) NH JF DL MA VR NM SBU OW
Date: 2004–ongoing

Four Seasons Hotel Rooftop Spa

The Four Seasons Park Lane, built in 1969, was the first five star metropolitan hotel of the hotelier Isadore Sharp who had turned from architecture to motel owner and builder in downtown Toronto the stepping stone to a worldwide brand. By 2004 it was tired and John Stauss had the idea with Mar Sharp of turning the roof, the private preserve of the hotel engineers into a spa. The old team of Susan Harmsworth of Espa with whom we worked on the Mandarin Oriental Spa (Volume 1) began work in 2004. The idea was to create a cornice or edge that floats above a glass wall containing the treatment rooms.

C: Hisham Abdulrahman Jaffer and Four Seasons Hotel Group
M&E: Industrial Design Associates
SE: AKT
QS: Gleeds
EPA Team: EP RB JO* RC SF GC AM GH JAS
Date: 2004–ongoing

Lyall Mews Residence

We were invited by Chester Jones, the interior designer, to join him in the complex reordering if the ground floor and basement levels of a Thomas Cubitt House and its associated mews building. Architecturally the most significant move was the creation of a single stair between the two parts to allow the length of the site at just under 40 m to be understood as a continuous sequence of spaces. Concrete blades support exposed in-situ concrete floors. The mews building retains its rather severe working character eschewing the tweeness of the local authority's design guide. The restricted inner court spaces are to be landscaped by Christopher Bradley-Hole.

C: Private Client
M&E: Michael Popper Associates
SE: Michael Hadi Associates
QS: LG Consult Ltd
ID: Chester Jones
Lands: Christopher Bradley-Hole
A: EP RC* TS GC CH RL BB
Date: 2005–ongoing

Lipton Residence

Seventeen years ago the ambition was to design a contemporary new build villa to replace the existing lacklustre 1930s neo-Queen Anne house. This was thwarted by the combined resistance of Camden and the Eyre Estate. Submitting to the conservationist view we gutted the house retaining key structural elements and modified the garden elevation (Volume 1). We are now submitting for planning a new build villa designed to Code 4 sustainability standards to reflect the generational shift in family requirements. The calm of the stuccoed street facade supported by concrete pillars and floating above a glazed ground floor ribbon transforms into a series of liberated cubic extensions that open up to the garden. The dormered attic is replaced by a large family space for a growing number of grandchildren reflecting 40 years of occupation.

C: Private Client
M&E / SE: Arup
QS: Davis Langdon
A: EP RK* ZF TS
Date: 2005–ongoing

7 & 8 St James's Square

We won an invited competition to design a replacement building for the corner of St James' Square and Duke of York Street and integrate the adjoining building 7 St James' Square. 7 St James' Square is an elegantly proportioned and detailed townhouse designed by Edwin Lutyens in 1911 for the three bachelor Farrer brothers of banking fame had become the headquarters of the Royal Fine Art Commission until it was replaced by The Commission for Architecture and the Built Environment (CABE) in 1999. The design for 8 St James' Square, to replace the ill proportioned existing building, is a carefully crafted contemporary brick elevation to the square to echo the original scale and detailing of the square most closely exemplified in 9 St James' Square to the immediate west side of Duke of York Street. On the eve of demolition the site was sold and for the time being the square was robbed of the chance to improve this important corner.

C: Britel Fund Trustees and Hermes Real Estate
DM: City & West End
M&E: Hilson Moran Partnership
SE: Price & Myers
QS: EC Harris
A: EP NJ PC* ER DC ZF JAS OW
Date: 2005–2007

Selfridges Entrances

Gordon Selfridge dreamed of a store stretching from Oxford Street to Wigmore Street with a dome as large as St Paul's Cathedral and a frontage, as built, from Duke Street to Orchard Street. The IRA bombed the Oxford Street windows in December 1974 and the smaller replacement windows were a compromise. Our redesign of the shop windows and entrances brings back their original scale and recreates the grandeur of the ground floor elevations. The full-height glass, new lighting and stage works reflect the innovative shop displays that are an attraction in their own right. Extensive research in the company's fascinating archive of drawings and photographs together with site investigations of remaining original details have informed our detailing. The reinstatement of the awnings remains an ambition which would significantly improve the quality of the public realm along Oxford Street.

C: Selfridges Retail Ltd
M&E: Troup Bywaters & Anders
SE: Alan Baxter & Associates
QS: Davis Langdon
A: RK JO* MA
Date: 2005–ongoing

Chelsfield London

When Sir Stuart Lipton left Stanhope EPA helped locate and fit out his new executive offices in Mayfair. The space on the third floor of two post-war buildings has a simple L-shaped plan with excellent daylighting to its shallow depth. The reception area and internal circulation are day lit through the glazed partitions to the executive and meeting rooms. The monochromatic scheme is structured with large photographic prints of iconic twentieth century architectural settings on panels and doors. The bright upholstery of the Eames chairs and the clients art collection bring colour to each interior. Recessed ceiling light slots, light casing to the structural columns and integral wall storage mischievously order the awkward condition into a flowing sequence of spaces. The executive rooms are designed and furnished to have dual use for both individual desk work and small meetings.

C: Chelsfield
M&E: Arup Engineering
QS: Davis Langdon
A: EP RK* GH
Date: 2006

Mana Residence

Our client bought the decaying Notting Hill end of terrace building, formerly a warehouse and builders yard, and gave us a brief for domestic spaces and the requirements to house an extensive contemporary art collection including sculpture, large pictures and video works. The site is hemmed in by neighbours and the key to the design was to create a top-lit interior garden as the focus of the multi-levelled house. The scheme will create a highly energy efficient, eccentric and imaginative solution to a compromised urban site. The addition of the mews building creates a surreal juxtaposition of spatial and entrance scales.

C: Private Client
M&E: Michael Popper Associates
SE: Michael Hadi Associates
QS: LG Consult
EPA Team: EP RLL*
Date: 2006–ongoing

Babcock & Brown London

Occupying four floors of our city building 5 Aldermanbury Square, the fit-out for Babcock & Brown is on floor 12–15. The reception is conceived as a 'studio' space, as a neutral envelope for creative uses. The ceiling is stripped exposing the steel structure and walls clad with pressed metal panels backed by acoustic felt lining house the services. Sliding panels accommodate art work and special surfaces. The space, capable of accommodating the entire working community is a forum and reception and looks southward to the iconic chimney of Tate Modern. The four floors are connected by a highly crafted suspended spiral stair. On the floor below the central section provides common break out spaces.

C: Babcock & Brown
M&E: Hilson Moran Partnership
SE: Whitbybird
QS: Bigham Anderson
A: EP NJ MC* RLL AM JAS
Date: 2006–2007

120 Fenchurch Street

This joint venture proposes the redevelopment on a whole urban block on the north side of Fenchurch Street at the heart of the City of London's insurance district. A lengthy series of massing and design proposals were developed and reviewed with the planning officers. Despite being close to the apex of the City's proposed tall buildings the option for an elegant tower was dismissed in favour of an urban block proposal. The scale, at 15-storeys, is modulated in section with the separation of canted upper floor levels from the main block. The plan form is also faceted to create engaging views of the building form the sweeping Fenchurch Street. In contrast to the monotony of the metal and glass cladding of the surrounding buildings the main facade is clad with light ceramic fins. The upper level glazing and solar shades to the lower floors have coloured glass and metal. A public vote passed through the building at street level and at its mid point dramatic views of the sky are framed. Piercing this void are two tilted public lifts that run directly to the roof where the whole of the roof is to be a public accessible garden offering panoramic views in every direction.

C: Babcock & Brown
M&E: Waterman Building Services
SE: Whitbybird
QS: Northcroft
A: EP RK* ARM DL SF NA
Date: 2006–ongoing

Timothy Taylor Gallery Carlos Place

The second Timothy Taylor Gallery in Carlos Place, Mayfair, opened its doors with a show by renowned post-war American painter, Alex Katz. The light and elegant gallery sits within the shell of a former bank building located just off Grosvenor Square in the Mayfair Conservation Area. The space is designed as a neutral backdrop to the art on display and can accommodate very large 2-D and 3-D works of art. The scheme includes viewing rooms, office space, painting storage, staff facilities and a workshop. Spread over ground and lower ground floors, the public and private areas are linked by a solid oak staircase.

C: Timothy Taylor Gallery
SE: Michael Hadi Associates
QS: LG Consult
A: EP CH* TS
Date: 2006–2007

The Selfridge Hotel

The Selfridge Hotel is located at the northwest corner of the Selfridges' urban block situated on the north side of Oxford Street. The Hotel will be completely refurbished with a new reception, public areas, guest rooms and back of house areas, making a significant improvement to the existing facilities.

The proposal involves opening up the ground floor entrance aspect with a new lightweight canopy which allows the hotel entrance to be viewed from the street and a new glazed entrance area creating a dramatic arrival lobby. The first floor will house the hotel bar, lounge, meeting rooms and restaurant areas. The restaurant having a new external terrace over the existing flat roof.

Set within the garden terrace a new pavilion will provide accommodation for suites and will address the street, marking the entrance and the new Selfridge Hotel.

C: Selfridges & Co.
M&E: Faber Maunsell
SE: Buro Happold
QS: Davis Langdon
LA: Todd Longstaffe-Gowan
ID: MBDS
A: EP LH* SF ARM HA YK BL
Date: 2006–ongoing

Timothy Taylor Table

There have been a number of pieces of one-off furniture in previous projects—the dining table at the Chateau de Paulin, the stainless steel hall table for Capener's Close—and there is a desire now to move closer to product design where there is the opportunity. Timothy Taylor commissioned a table for his art fair spaces. The brief was for a table that had presence and was to be big enough to show books and to be able to meet potential clients, or for two staff to sit at. The art fairs are far flung and the table was therefore to be dismantlable, like the tradition of military campaign or expedition furniture. The table has a split top in Corian and single stainless steel leg and armature and one pier to lend stability.

C: Timothy Taylor Gallery
A: EP TP* RLL
Date: 2006

Cedars Hall, Wells Cathedral School

The school specialises in both vocal and instrumental music. The new recital hall and practice spaces will provide a much needed physical heart to the school set between the listed Cedars House and the listed landscape which surrounds the school's sports field. The gallery overlooking the performance space is at the level of the fields, entry to the building is via a gentle ramp arcing adjacent to an ancient yew hedge. The height of the hall required for acoustics is reflected in the floating roof structure—raising the roof—and the walls are externally a juxtaposition of singular rusted metal panels and massive glazed panels. There are a number of landscape and smaller buildings that are annotated with the project. The school is currently fundraising.

C: Wells Cathedral School
M&E: Buro Happold
SE: Momentum Consulting Engineers
QS: Faithful + Gould
A: EP CH JAS*
Date: 2007

Staff List

The order of initials reflects design responsibility * marks project team leader. Where this was passed on between design (1) and construction (2) the * is followed by respective figure.

References for Design Team:
C   Client
PM   Project Manager
SE   Structural Engineer
M&E   Mechanical Engineering Consultants
QS   Quantity Surveyor
LA   Landscape Architect
A   EPA Architects

EP   Eric Parry
b. 1952, BA hons Newcastle 1973, MARCA 1978
founded practice in 1983

RK   Robert Kennett
b. 1964, BA hons 1986, DipArch Cantab 1989
worked at EPA from 1989 to present
appointed director in 1997

NJ   Nick Jackson
b. 1964, BA hons 1986, DipArch Cantab 1989
worked at EPA from 1990 to present
appointed director in 1997

JS   Justin Sayer
b. 1960, BA 1982, Bsc 1992, DipArch UCL 1995
worked at EPA from 1996 to present
appointed associate in 2003
appointed associate director in 2007

RB   Roz Barr
b. 1969, BA hons 1991, MA Design 1993, DipArch UCL 1999
worked at EPA from 2000 to present
appointed associate in 2003
appointed associate director in 2007

NL   Nigel Lea
b. 1966, BA hons 1988, DipArch Edin 1992
worked at EPA from 1999–2007
appointed associate in 2003

Architects

AVO	Alvaro Valdivia a l'Onions	IL	Imogen Long	PF	Peter Ferretto
ARM	Anil Mistry	JL	Jan Loerhs	PC	Phil Clarke
AM	Aya Maeda	JP	Janna Posiadly	RD	Robert Dawson
BB	Ben Burley	JSA	Jane Sanders	RH	Robert Hirschfield
BH	Ben Hassell	JF	Jeremy Foster	RK	Robert Kennett
BL	Brenda Leonard	JO	Julian Ogiwara	RCO	Roberta Colombo
BD	Brendan Durkin	JAS	Julie Stewart	RL	Roo Lam Lau
CH	Christine Humphreys	JD	Juliet Davis	RC	Ros Cohen
CB	Christopher Burton	JSC	Juliette Scalbert	RB	Roz Barr
CT	Claudia Tschunko	JS	Justin Sayer	SB	Sam Brougham
DL	Damien Lee	LM	Laura Miller	SBU	Simon Buss
DK	David Kahn	LH	Lee Higson	SF	Sofia Ferreira
DM	Denitza Moreau	LME	Lina Meister	SW	Stephen Witherford
DC	Douglas Carson	LN	Lisa Ngan	SM	Susanna Miller
ET	Emma Tubbs	MK	Mark Kelly	TP	Tanya Parkin
EP	Eric Parry	MR	Martin Reynolds	TS	Tao Sule
ER	Eva Ravnborg	MC	Merit Claussen	TT	Taro Tsuruta
FE	Felipe Errazuriz	ML	Michael Lane	TO	Thorsten Overberg
FP	Freddie Phillipson	MA	Mohammed Ageli	TL	Tim Lynch
GH	Gert Halbgebauer	NA	Nan Atichatpong	VR	Vania Ramos
GC	Gonzalo Coello Perez	NM	Neil Mathews	YK	Yamac Korfali
GP	Guy Parkinson	NH	Nicholas Hornig	ZF	Ze'ev Feigis
HA	Hayley Anderson	NJ	Nick Jackson		
IA	India Aspin	NL	Nigel Lea		
		OW	Owen Watson		

Non architectural staff
Cat Robson
Catherine Harrington
Chloe Robinson
Clare O'Regan
Diane Kurup
Elaine Labram
Emma Tracey
Gabriella Gullberg
Jacqui Barhouch
Jake Bailey
James Young
Jin Georgiou
Julia Wedegaertner
Julie Reynolds
Karen Cheung
Kira Aujla
Laura Houston
Nieven Kadry
Parveen Abdulraman
Rolandas Simkevicius
Ruth Lepper
Shea Jordan-Hawkins
Sue Flint

Photo Credits

Cover. BS

5. TS

Introduction

6. NK
11. JM
12. NJ
15. AP
16. CR
21. TS
26. AP

30 Finsbury Square

32. HB
37. HB
38. DL
39. DL
40. HBG
41. HB (bottom left and top left)
43. HB (left and bottom right)
43. PC (top right)
44. PC
45. HB
46. HB
47. HB

Old Wardour House

48. NK
50. SA
51. NK
55. NK
57. NK

Hamilton Terrace

58. TS
60. NK
61. TS
62. TS
64. TS
67. TS
68. TS
69. TS

Royal Lancaster Hotel

70. NK
75. NK
76. NK
77. NK
79. NK

Paternoster Square

80. NK
86. CP
87. CP
90. NK
91. NK

Bedford School Library

92. PC
94. PC
99. PC
101. PC
102. PC
103. PC

Bedford Music School

104. HB
107. HB
110. PC (left)
110. HB (right)
111. HB
112. HB (left)
112. PC (right)
113. HB
115. HB

Wimbledon School of Art

116. NK
121. NK
122. NK
124. NK
125. NK

Timothy Taylor Gallery

126. NK
128. NK
129. NK
130. NK
131. NK
132. NK
133. NK

Park Street

134. Smoothe
136. AP
139. AP (bottom)
141. AP
141. Modelmaker: Network Modelmakers

Aldermanbury Square

142. MF
144. Smoothe
145. TS (left)
145. HB (right)
146. AP
146. Modelmaker: Kandor
147. AP
147. Modelmaker: Weird Dimensions
149. TS (left)
149. HB (right)
151. TS
153. TS
154. MF
156. TS
157. TS
159. HB

Three Offices

160. NK
162. NK
164. NK
165. NK
166. NK
167. NK

St Martin-in-the-Fields

168. GS
170. GS
187. GS
172. CS (except left middle)
175. AP
182. Modelmaker: Weird Dimensions
182. AP
187. GS

Modelmakers

Weird Dimensions
Kandor
Network Modelmakers

Photographers

Balthazar Serreau — BS
Timothy Soar — TS
Nicholas Kane — NK
John Mitchell — JM
Nick Jackson — NJ
Andrew Putler — AP
Claudia Renetzki — CR
Hélène Binet — HB
Dirk Lellau — DL
HBG Construction — HBG
Peter Cook/View — PC
Salisbury Archive — SA
Cristobal Palma — CP
Max Fenton — MF
Chris Steele-Perkins/Magnum — CS
Grant Smith — GS

Acknowledgements

Volume 2 covers a period of six years from the publication of Volume 1 in 2002. Volume 1 ended with Hélène Binet's photograph of the latent power of a freshly quarried Portland stone block, which was incorporated in the elevation of 30 Finsbury Square. This project as a completed building opens Volume 2. Grant Smith's image of anticipation in the frozen clock face of St Martin-in-the-Fields ends this volume.

The endeavour got off to a wonderful start because both Wilfried Wang and Dalibor Vesely agreed with little hesitation to repeat their respective contributions once more. Wilfried Wang has written in his introductory essay with extraordinary prescience about the consequences of the fiscal decadence of the Anglo Saxon banking system (almost two years ahead of the crash of 2008). Intriguingly he parallels this state of affairs with the moribund condition of architectural theory and criticism in the UK. Reading his text and the way he draws on a vast perspective and knowledge one can understand his frustration and his own position. Dalibor Vesely's introductory text is both a reflection on the work but also a sharp reminder of what our goals should be. I feel the deepest gratitude that these two exceptional and important voices in the world of architecture today have considered the body of work worthwhile scrutinising.

I have written covering texts for a few projects which were either unbuilt, Park Street, or not visited by Wilfried Wang and myself, Wimbledon School of Arts, or a group of smaller projects, three London offices.

Two particular personal thanks are to Peter Carl for the generosity of time and thought in a continual encouraging presence. The same is true albeit at a greater distance of David Leatherbarrow.

In the office many friends have passed through and made contributions. Architecture has an elephantine gestation period and many of these projects are five year plus endeavours. The book would not exist without the dedication and patience of Aya Maeda who was responsible for all the line drawings, rebuilding most from the plethora of detail in technical files, and Jacqui Barhouch and Gabriella Gullberg who has kept an exemplary control of detail coordinating both the written and photographic work.

I would like to thank a number of people who have written elsewhere about the projects in this volume: Ed Jones and Eddie Heathcote on Finsbury Square; Jeremy Melvin and Ellis Woodman on the Bedford School Library and Ellis for the Bedford Music School; Bob Allies and Jay Merrick on Aldermanbury Square; Ken Powell on Paternoster Square; Jeremy Melvin on Old Wardour House; Peter Brades on Wimbledon School of Art and Stephen Bayley on the proposals for St Martin-in-the-Fields.

I am aware this volume is being published later than anticipated. I am thankful to Duncan McCorquodale for his patience and for the designers at Black Dog, particularly Emilia Gomez, Julia Trudeau Rivest and Matt Bucknall.

Colophon

© 2011 Black Dog Publishing Limited, London, UK, the architect and authors.
All rights reserved.

Black Dog Publishing Limited
10A Acton Street
London WC1X 9NG

t. +44 (0) 207 713 5097
f. +44 (0) 207 713 8682
e. info@blackdogonline.com

Designed at BDP.

All opinions expressed within this publication are those of the authors and not necessarily of the publisher.

British Library Cataloguing-in-Publication Data.
A CIP record for this book is available from the British Library.

ISBN 978 1 906155 25 4

No part of this publication may be reproduced, stored in a retrieval system, or transmitted, in any form or by any means, electronic, mechanical, photocopying, recording, or otherwise, without prior permission of Black Dog Publishing Limited.

Every effort has been made to trace the copyright holders, but if any have been inadvertently overlooked, the necessary arrangements will be made at the first opportunity.

Black Dog Publishing Limited, London, UK, is an environmentally responsible company. *Eric Parry Architects Volume 2* is printed on FSC certified paper.

Printed in China by Everbest.

Also available *Eric Parry Architects Volume 1*
ISBN: 978 1 906155 62 9

architecture art design
fashion history photography
theory and things

www.blackdogonline.com

black dog publishing
london uk